Passover

The Story of Easter from the Beginning

Nathan Slegers

 comethirstyministry.com

Dedicated to my wife Alicia,

my partner in ministry, and soulmate.

Contents

Preface

It's often said that the Bible is one story from beginning to end—a story of redemption. I couldn't agree more. Yet our biblical instruction is rarely done that way. Sermon series often cover month-long topical issues or emphasize a particular person or story such as Moses or the Exodus. Done this way, stories such as the Exodus are investigated in isolation and when the story is over, a new topic begins. But what about the rest of the "one" story?

The Passover and Easter (and all the connections in between) are best told as one story rather than as two separate ones. This pairing is certainly one of those cases where the entirety is greater than the sum of the parts. The philosophy behind this book is to take familiar stories such as the Exodus, Isaac and Rebekah, Joshua, Ruth, and the Triumphant Entry and to organize them as pieces of a larger puzzle.

My hope is that this perspective will enrich the redemption story that you think you know with new depth and appreciation. In essence, the goal is that "the peace of God, which transcends all understanding, will guard your hearts and your minds in Christ Jesus" (Philippians 4:7). By that, I mean we already have an understanding of the individual stories, but, when woven together as one, the complete story provides a new peace that transcends the parts.

This book can certainly be read at any time of the year, but since it walks through the history of redemption, culminating in Easter, it's particularly well-suited for the Lenten season. Lent is a season of forty days, not counting Sundays, which begins on Ash Wednesday and ends on Holy Saturday, the day before Easter. Lent is a time of repentance, fasting, reflection, and preparation for the coming of Easter. The material in this book is easily broken into six parts, one for each full week of Lent. Finishing the final chapter just before Palm Sunday will hopefully refresh your soul and prepare your heart for Easter. My suggested outline for such a study is as follows:

> Week 1 – Chapters 1 and 2
> Week 2 – Chapter 3
> Week 3 – Chapter 4
> Week 4 – Chapter 5
> Week 5 – Chapter 6
> Week 6 – Chapter 8 (Optionally, include Chapter 7)

This material is especially well-suited for group studies. The connections between Passover and Easter are numerous, and it wasn't my intention to exhaustively cover them all. As a result, there is ample room for group discussions as readers may find their own connections left unexplored here.

Regardless if you are taking this journey by yourself or with a group, I am eager for you to revisit some familiar stories with the goal of refreshing the redemption story as we watch the Passover unfold, from the beginning of creation, into the story of Easter.

- One -

Puzzle Pieces

And beginning with Moses and all the Prophets, he explained to them what was said in all the Scriptures concerning himself.

Luke 24:27

It's been almost a decade since my pastor at the time invited a Messianic rabbi to speak at our church one Sunday morning. He came in preparation for an evening Messianic Passover meal, called a Seder, which he would lead us through to illustrate some of the Jewish connections to Jesus.

His premise was simple. He linked the sacrifice of a lamb without defect to provide redemption from Pharaoh at the first Passover with Jesus, the spotless Lamb of God, who was also sacrificed at Passover to provide our redemption. This is familiar ground for most of us. Something we've heard preached many times.

However, in the midst of this familiarity, he mentioned some details that I'd never before connected. He started by identifying the prescribed timing of the selection, inspection, and sacrifice of the Passover lambs in the twelfth chapter of Exodus. The precise instructions were to happen on specific days of the month. Next, he reconstructed the days leading up to the crucifixion and showed that they aligned with the twelfth chapter of Exodus. Jesus and the Passover lambs were brought to Jerusalem at the same time, inspected together, and then sacrificed. The facts were not new to me, yet having both events overlaid and shown to match so closely seemed momentous.

As I later asked around, there were people who, like me, were not aware of these connections. And yet others were aware. It made me ask, "How many other connections were known about which no one ever told me?" And, just as importantly, "Are there any connections that may have begun to evaporate from common knowledge over the decades?"

First Connections

I immediately started searching for other connections between the early Passovers and the final week of Jesus's ministry. Very quickly, links between Moses, the Exodus, and Jesus became apparent.

One of the first I discovered was Luke connecting Jesus and Moses in a significant way, which only appears as a footnote in most Bibles. In Luke's account of the transfiguration we read: "Two men, Moses and Elijah, appeared in glorious splendor, talking with Jesus. They spoke about his *departure*, which he was about to bring to fulfillment at Jerusalem" (Luke 9:30-31, emphasis added). The word "departure" is the translation of the Greek word *exodus*.[1] It's a subtle link, but using my paraphrase, one could read it as, "Moses and Jesus spoke of Jesus's exodus, which he was about to bring to fulfillment at Jerusalem." Both Moses and Jesus having an *exodus* seems significant.

The words Jesus chose to use at the Last Supper also connect that week to Moses and the first Passover. God told the Israelites before leaving Egypt, "This is a day you are to *commemorate*; for the *generations to come* you shall celebrate it as a festival to the

LORD—a lasting ordinance" (Exodus 12:14, emphasis added). Compare this to Jesus's words:

> *And he took bread, gave thanks and broke it, and gave it to them, saying, "This is my body given for you; do this in remembrance of me." In the same way, after the supper he took the cup, saying, "This cup is the new covenant in my blood, which is poured out for you."*
>
> Luke 22:19-20

At this Passover Jesus also declares, "Do this in remembrance of me," meaning, commemorate this Passover. Even more striking are the symbols of the covenant. Jesus marks the new covenant with wine representing his blood. Similarly, "Moses then took the blood, sprinkled it on the people and said, 'This is the blood of the covenant that the LORD has made with you in accordance with all these words'" (Exodus 24:8).

The connections between the first Passover and this one run deep. Both tell of redemption: one within an old covenant; the other by defining a new covenant. The purpose in Jesus's declaration was to link his words and actions to the Old Testament and to establish a unity of purpose in his ministry and in the entire history of redemption.

After the resurrection, the events on the road to Emmaus that opened this chapter (Luke 24:27) provide another significant connection. Any doubts that the Passion of Christ was not included in the ancient prophecies are put to rest with this grand declaration.

EXTRA DIMENSIONS

Once one starts looking for connections, you become hypersensitive to those ideas. Subtleties that you once would've overlooked now become triggers for thought.

After becoming aware of these first few connections, whenever the Exodus, Passover, or redemption came up in books, sermons, and studies, I paid special attention. I found that once I started asking, "Where does the Passover appear?", its richness and depth started appearing in unexpected places. It reminded me of those Magic Eye[2] books that came out in the '90s. They were full of abstract pictures and dots that you would stare at for a while until a three-dimensional image would appear from out of the two-dimensional page. It took some effort, but the reward was the appearance of a remarkable image with extra depth, an image that otherwise would be absent to a casual observer. An important distinction here is that the three-dimensional image was intentionally designed into the picture by the designer and was not just an anomaly created by an imaginative observer, like seeing animal shapes in passing clouds.

The redemption of the Passover and Old Testament were obviously intimately connected to the redemption of the New Testament. However, many times I'd heard it presented as simply comparing the Passover of the Exodus to the new covenant defined by Jesus at the Last Supper. Was it really that plain? Was redemption shown at the Exodus then figuratively put into hibernation until Jesus completed redemption and later explained it in the New Testament? Most know that's not how it happened, yet, at the same time, in this generation of thirty-minute sermons it often comes across that way.

The gospel is an amazingly rich message that is simple while also having extreme depth. A recent book by Jayson Georges called *The 3D Gospel*[3] discusses the depth to which sin is viewed across different cultures. He explores three different perspectives of the same gospel, namely: guilt-innocence, shame-honor, and fear-power perspectives.[4] Each facet uses different terminology when discussing redemption. The guilt-innocence perspective speaks of law, justice, and sacrifice. The shame-honor view often uses words such as loyalty, approval, and inheritance, while the fear-power perspective highlights triumph, oppression, and prayer.

These different facets of the same gospel give it richness and appeal to different people and cultures in unique ways. A good example of how Paul uses all three occurs in Ephesians where he says:

> In him we have redemption through his blood, the **forgiveness** of sins, ... I pray that the eyes of your heart may be enlightened in order that you may know the hope to which he has called you, the riches of his glorious **inheritance** in his holy people, and his incomparably great power for us who believe. That **power is the same as the mighty strength** he exerted ...
>
> Ephesians 1:7a, 18-20a, emphasis added

If the redemption of the new covenant has such depth, what about the redemption of the old covenant? As we'll find in the following chapters, the redemption of the Old Testament, which helps establish the depth of the gospel, is not "flat" at all. Rather, it has remarkable depth, and its connection to the gospel message will bring more dimensions to both.

COMPLETING A PUZZLE

The purpose of this book is to take a fresh look at the connection between Passover and Easter. We'll collect pieces of the puzzle as we explore all of scripture, much like an investigator trying to solve a mystery. As with any puzzle, often the best place to start is with the corner pieces, and then to proceed to the edges. From that point the entire puzzle begins to take shape. Similarly, we'll start with some fundamental corners—a summary of the gospel and the Exodus—from which we can fill in the edges.

Many of the pieces we'll look at are very familiar but are still helpful to revisit as we connect the dots between the Passover and Easter. However, some of the pieces may be completely new to many as we connect them to the Passover. Stories such as Joshua only quickly mention Passover while, Ruth doesn't even use the word at all. Yet both will provide rich depth to the Passover as they point toward Easter.

Finally, I want to emphasize that while connections and facts will make up the bulk of our investigation, they are not the ultimate point. What good is it to be knowledgeable about redemption as outlined from the Passover to Easter if it doesn't change your life? Therefore, each chapter will end with a section titled "What do I do with it?" It's intended to revisit the information we've uncovered, but from a *life* perspective, and to provide a catalyst to think about how it could change your relationships with others and with God.

So let's begin our investigation of Passover—the story of Easter from the beginning.

- Two -

What's in a Name?

Restore to me the joy of your salvation and grant me a
willing spirit, to sustain me.

Psalm 51:12

One Saturday, my daughter Adeline, who was seven at the time, and I were driving to the hardware store. She was sitting next to me in the front of our truck when she asked: "Dad, how do you know you're driving in the lines? I can't see the lines on the road, and it looks like the front of the truck goes over them. How do you know that you won't get hit by the cars coming toward us?"

It was a very clever question since, indeed, when you look over the hood or fenders, the lines in the road and nearby vehicles are obscured by the truck. At least from our perspective.

At first I chuckled at this simple question. But then, as I tried to form a good answer to satisfy my curious daughter, I realized maybe the answer was not going to be that easy after all. What I quickly recognized was that I was so familiar with driving that I never thought consciously about where the edge of my truck actually was compared to the lines in the road. And the more I thought about it, I couldn't recall anybody ever showing or explaining to me that the projection of my hood was not where the wheels or bumper would be. It was just something I picked up from experience. Over time I had become so *familiar* with the idea, that I now took it for granted.

That familiarity with the principle made it challenging to explain to my daughter. Eventually I came up with a contorted explanation, which seemed to settle the issue in her mind. At least, it settled it enough that she hasn't felt it necessary to ask her dad again.

THE LAMB OF GOD

Many things in our daily lives, professions, and our Christian faith can reach that same level of familiarity. They can become familiar to the point that we take them for granted and often struggle with the reasons we know and trust those principles.

One such Christian principle, a common name for Jesus, occurs at the opening of John's gospel. "The next day John saw Jesus coming toward him and said, 'Look, the *Lamb of God*, who takes away the sin of the world!'" (John 1:29). If you've grown up in the Church or even have just been around the Church, the "Lamb of God" is likely a very familiar name. It's a prolific phrase and a common theme that appears in many traditional songs, such as "Are You Washed in the Blood" and "Just as I Am."

But what does the name Lamb of God really mean? The simple answer is that it connects the crucifixion (and the subsequent resurrection) to the Passover in Exodus and the atonement sacrifices instated in the Pentateuch. While that answer may be correct, it also seems quite sterile and void of the emotion that John the Baptist intended when he announced Jesus as "the

Lamb of God, who takes away the sin of the world!"

Are we so familiar with the name "Lamb of God" that we take it for granted? Does it still invoke all the meaning and still stir our passions like John the Baptist intended centuries ago? I have to admit, there are times when the name "Lamb of God" occurs in songs or sermons so often that I'm almost dismissive of it. Not because I don't recognize its importance, but because it's so often used.

That's not to say that it's overused. There are good reasons why the Lamb of God is cited so frequently in Christian circles. Let's look at a few.

If you had to summarize the gospel very concisely to someone, how would you go about it? I suggest, based on the three sections of scripture below (although there are many others we could also use), that we can form a solid, yet concise, foundation.

For all have sinned and fall short of the glory of God, and all are justified freely by his grace through the redemption that came by Christ Jesus. God presented Christ as a sacrifice of atonement, through the shedding of his blood—to be received by faith. Romans 3:23-25

For what I received I passed on to you as of first importance: that Christ died for our sins according to the Scriptures, that he was buried, that he was raised on the third day according to the Scriptures. 1 Corinthians 15:3-4

For it is by grace you have been saved, through faith—and this is not from yourselves, it is the gift of God—not by works, so that no one can boast. Ephesians 2:8-9

Pulling together the ideas from above, the gospel may be summarized as, "We have all sinned, redemption comes from the death and resurrection of Christ Jesus, it's a gift of God, which is accepted through faith." That's a very good summary of the gospel, and, while some may find nuances they would clarify, I contend that most Christians would accept that summary. What's more, these four gospel elements, just distilled from these seven verses, are also summarized very well by the name the "Lamb of God." That one name covers aspects of the Passover and the atonement sacrifices, who does the work and why, and how we are to engage in redemption—all without needing to dive into complex theology or Old Testament rituals.

In English the names for Passover and Easter put up an artificial divide between the two events which unintentionally masks the intimate connection between the two. The origin of the English (and German) name for Easter is from the pagan goddess of spring and fertility, Eostre. However, when we look at almost all other languages, the intimate connection between Passover and Easter can be seen. When God told Moses and Aaron about the final plague and how blood on their doors would allow the plague to passover them, he declared "… it is the LORD's Passover" (Exodus 12:11). In Hebrew, the word for the Passover is *Pesach*. Most languages refer to Easter by names derived from the Hebrew name for Passover,[1] Examples include *Pascha* in Latin, *Pâques* in French, and *Paskha* in Russian. Easter and Passover are two events that are really just parts of one story, sometimes referred to as the "Paschal Mystery" —a term describing redemption and the events of the Last Supper and Passion, which reach their climax on Easter Sunday.

John the Baptist's main emphasis of proclaiming Jesus as the Lamb of God may have been to connect the Passover to Jesus. In doing so, he linked the substitutionary sacrifice of the Passover to Jesus and what he would soon fulfill through his death and resurrection, which we celebrate as Easter. The declaration "Lamb of God" keenly connects both Passover and Easter and everything in between through one remarkable name. "Lamb of God" may be used prolifically and be all too familiar to us, but that's justified by the breadth it spans and by its importance.

THAT'S YOUR PLAN?

Familiarity with the Lamb of God that connects Passover and Easter is certainly desirable, yet it can bring a detrimental side effect. When we become intimately familiar with a place or idea, it's more challenging to appreciate the nuances and complexity, and, in some cases, we may even miss the significance.

The Disciples fell into this state of familiarity as the final Passover of Jesus's ministry approached. They were certainly knowledgeable about the Passover tradition and the Old Testament prophets. Even more, they had a front row seat to Jesus's ministry. Yet as the Lamb of God approached Jerusalem for his last Passover, they were so close to the events that they "… did not understand all this" (John 12:16). They knew the details, but when presented with their fulfillment they missed it and at that point wouldn't be able to explain it to others. "Only after Jesus was glorified did they realize that these things had been written about him" (John 12:16). What the Disciples were missing at that moment was the continuous link between the Passover and the events to come, culminating in Easter.

Imagine bringing someone to your church who has never been exposed to mainstream Christianity. Depending on your church and the week, they may hear ideas about redeeming blood, Jesus's blood being poured out for us, God's perfect Son being sacrificed, and possibly even the Lamb of God. To us these phrases seem natural and obvious, but to others the idea of blood sacrifices seems archaic and bizarre. Even more, the idea that killing your son would help resolve any problem, no matter how large, seems even more outlandish to modern ears.

To many secular people, the entire idea of "Christ as a sacrifice of atonement, through the shedding of his blood" (Romans 3:25) is met with skepticism. The range of responses may span from polite dismissal to serious indignation. Paul was well-acquainted with the potential range of responses. As he pointed out: "For the message of the cross is foolishness to those who are perishing, but to us who are being saved it is the power of God. ... but we preach Christ crucified: a stumbling block to Jews and foolishness to Gentiles" (1Corinthians 1:18, 23). Many of the Jewish people at the time rejected the idea because either Jesus wasn't the type of savior they were expecting, or he wasn't the type of savior they wanted. For the Gentiles, the objection was often, "you are bringing some strange ideas to our ears" (Acts 17:20). In both cases, the continuous link between the Passover and Easter was not made.

Paul confronted this skepticism on many occasions, and it's remarkable how people have not changed much in their responses to the gospel over the last two millennia. In Athens, Paul met philosophers (an ancient version of our modern-day intellectuals) who, in essence, mocked him personally by name-calling, saying, "what is this babbler saying" and "sneering" at the idea of the resurrection (Acts 17:18,32). However, in Berea, they too were skeptical, but at least they examined Paul's message with great eagerness and searched the scriptures to verify for themselves whether what Paul was preaching was true (Acts 17:10-12). In both Athens and Berea, Paul was allowed to present his argument to the people, and they chose their response. In other instances, Paul was met with worse than just skepticism. "They stoned Paul and dragged him outside the city, thinking he was dead" (Act 14:19). However, Paul was also remarkably resilient as he "got up and went back into the city" (Acts 14:20).

Times really haven't changed much. Fortunately for most of us, stoning is an unlikely response (although in parts of our modern world, stoning is still a possible outcome.) However, just as Paul experienced, if someone asks you, "What is the reason for your belief?", be prepared for a healthy dose of skepticism.

For the most part, even modern secular society knows the basics tenets of the gospel that Paul was teaching. Even if they're not Christians, they know about the historical person of Jesus. Furthermore, it's likely they may know that Christianity claims Jesus died and was resurrected, which is supposed to provide forgiveness for our sins. That's not to say they believe it's true, but that at least they know the argument.

I'm naturally a skeptical person. I was one of those kids that always asked, "Why?" when people told me something. Not because I was questioning their authority, but because I have a natural curiosity about how things work. Many secular people are likewise skeptical of any religious claims. With regard to Christianity, their skepticism originates from basic philosophical questions about the Lamb of God. Often, from their perspective, Passover and Easter are no more than fictitious superstitions that evolved over time. A condescending statement I often hear is, "Do you actually belief that stuff?" It's a fair question that's best answered by first investigating some sources of their skepticism.

An article titled "10 Reasons the Crucifixion Story Makes No Sense" provides a good outline of the skepticism that modern secular people have about Christianity[2]. I obviously don't agree with the arguments proposed, but what is evident is that the author has a good understanding of the principles behind Passover and Easter. He lays out some very logical objections that essentially question the fundamental continuity between the two. These objections are the same objections that many people may have. To paraphrase his introduction:

Christians say that death by crucifixion was a horrible, humiliating way to die. That the death of Jesus was a tremendous sacrifice … and isn't it worth praising? Here are 10 reasons (we'll look at only 3) why I'm unimpressed:

Three of the author's best points are:

*We didn't do anything to get original sin. We inherited it from Adam. So why do we have to do anything to get redemption? If God demands a sacrifice, he got it. Why the requirement to **believe** to access the solution?* (Emphasis added.)

*If God loves us deeply and he wants to forgive us, **couldn't he just forgive us**? That's how we do it, and that's the lesson from the Prodigal Son where the father forgives the son even after being wronged by him.* (Emphasis added.)

***The story is incoherent**. God made mankind imperfect and inherently vulnerable to sin. But don't worry – God sacrificed Jesus, one of the persons of God (whatever that means), so mankind could go to heaven instead. So God sacrificed himself to himself so we could bypass a rule that God made himself and that God deliberately designed us to never be able to meet? I can't even understand that.* (Emphasis added.)

Many people have these or similar objections. A summary of these three arguments could be described as, "Why do I need faith?", "Why couldn't God just forgive us?", and "Why is the process so complicated?" It's the last question that I hear the most often. Once the entire story is laid out as the author does, many people start asking, "Why the drawn-out process?" Even those who accept the idea that Jesus had to be sacrificed as the Passover

Lamb then ask, "Why didn't God just start with the crucifixion at creation?"

Probably the most significant reason people see the entire story as potentially lacking coherence is that they view the crucifixion, centuries after Abraham and Moses, as God finally fixing a problem he knew about for a while but just could never find the time to address. That's simply not the case. We find that we "were *redeemed* from the empty way of life handed down to you from your ancestors, but with the precious blood of Christ, *a lamb without blemish or defect*. He was chosen *before the creation of the world, but was revealed in these last times* for your sake" (1Peter 1:18-20, emphasis added). We see that the Lamb of God was the plan from the beginning of creation.

I don't think God is insensitive to our desire for coherence. That may be one reason his redemptive plan, beginning with creation, declared in the Passover, and finished at Easter, was outlined over many centuries in detail. He knew that, for many of us, we don't do well with answers presented to us without lessons learned. We will always ask, "Why?" or, "Is there another way?" This just seems to be baked into humanity.

For those of us with young children we see this all the time. My oldest daughter, Ryann, always liked to be near her mom while she worked in the kitchen. I can vividly recall a time when she was about three years old and stood on a stool a few feet away and watched my wife, Alicia, make dinner on the stove. As Ryann became more curious, her hands would inch closer to the stove, and Alicia would say, "Ryann, the stove is hot, keep your hands away, or you will get burned." Ryann moved them back, but then, after a few minutes, it would start over again. "Ryann, the stove is hot, keep your hands away, or you will get burned." This happened four more times over a twenty-minute span. Then came the screaming! She touched the stove and burned her hand, and we spent the night in the emergency room.

Despite many clear warnings, she didn't take them seriously until she experienced the consequences. A decade later, Ryann has still never touched a hot stove again. Experience trumps advice. We adults aren't too different. If God would have just revealed his redemption plan in its entirety from the beginning, we would have never taken it seriously and always asked, "Couldn't it be done another way?"

Another reason God's redemptive plan may have been reveled over the centuries is articulated well by Daniel Peterson in his article "Defending the Faith: Are there any good reasons to believe?," where he says:

> *If God were to reveal himself fully and with unmistakable, irresistible clarity, that revelation would overwhelm and destroy our freedom. In his "Philosophical Fragments" (1844), Danish philosopher Soren Kierkegaard uses a parable about a king and a maiden to make this point: How can the king reveal his love to a women of humble parentage – given the huge disparity of rank, status and wealth between them – without coercing or crushing her?*
>
> *"Not to reveal oneself," he writes, "is the death of love, to reveal oneself is the death of the beloved." The only real choice open to the king is to court his beloved indirectly, by descending to her station, by taking on the character of a servant. So he disguises himself.* [3]

There's the aspect that God desires us to freely engage with him out of our own desire and love without being compelled. What many people are seeking is irrefutable evidence with which God overwhelms us, allowing belief with no rational alternative. No such evidence exists. If it did, it would crush our choice. However, God does provide us with sufficient information and whispers for those who are willing to listen.

ONE STORY FROM THE BEGINNING

The crucifixion and resurrection were not a root out of dry ground; it was alluded to, and hinted to, throughout scripture. Despite the Disciples and followers of Jesus struggling to fully comprehend what Jesus was explaining during his ministry, after the resurrection "beginning with Moses and all the Prophets, he explained to them what was said in all the scriptures concerning himself " (Luke 24:27).

John, the disciple whom Jesus loved, highlights the continuity and coherence of the gospel as he writes in his revelation, "I am the Alpha and the Omega, the First and the Last, the Beginning and the End" (Revelation 22:13). (Alpha and Omega are A and Ω, the first and last letters of the Greek alphabet, respectively.) Clearly, we can see the emphasis that the Lamb of God was chosen before creation and continues to eternity. Here John is emphasizing that the gospel is not the incoherent, ad hoc story some suggest, but spans from Genesis to Revelation, from beginning to end.

What's remarkable is that all the authors of scripture wrote their sections independently over centuries. Each was given a part, which by itself sometimes may have seemed out of place or difficult to comprehend at the time. However, when they are all told together, the result is the Lamb of God. The story was from the beginning even before it was written down.

As an example of how the story began to be revealed from the start, take some time to read the fifth chapter of Genesis. This genealogy from Adam to Noah is one of those chapters that most of us just rush through, as so-and-so became the father of so-and-so, etcetera. We commonly view this list of names as either just information for trivia or as a literary tool used to connect the story of Adam to the next story about Noah.

When investigating Hebrew genealogies it's important to note that the names aren't translated from their Hebrew roots. Rather, they are transliterated since the names are proper nouns. As an illustration, recall when God changed Abram's name and said, "your name will be Abraham, for I have made you a father of many nations" (Genesis 17:5). The word *ABRHM* in Hebrew literally means "father of many." However, when it is used as the name of Abraham, *ABRHM* is just transliterated as his name, "Abraham," rather than reading as, "Hey, you, 'father of many nations." A more modern comparison to us would be the name Sierra, which in Spanish means "mountains." When you name your child Sierra, you just call her "Sierra." You don't translate her name from Spanish and refer to her as "mountain." What's significant is that each Hebrew name in the genealogy in Genesis 5 has a root meaning that isn't translated in our English version.

Table 1. Genesis 5 Genealogy

Hebrew	English
Adam	*Man*
Seth	*Appointed*
Enosh	*Mortal*
Kenan	*Dwelling or Sorrow*[4]
Mahalalel	*The Glory of God*
Jared	*Shall Descend*
Enoch	*Teaching*
Methuselah	*His Death Shall Bring*
Lamech	*The Despairing*
Noah	*Rest or Comfort*

When we look at the first name in the genealogy, Adam (Genesis 5:1), the root of the word actually means "man" or "mankind" in Hebrew. This is not its first occurrence in Genesis. The word "adam" actually appears nine times[5] earlier in Genesis as either just "man" or "mankind" before it's first transliterated as the name Adam (Genesis 2:20). A similar analysis of the root meaning for each of the ten names in the genealogy is shown in Table 1, with the Hebrew transliteration on the left and the root meaning on the right.[6] If the ten names in the genealogy are read as a story, with some added conjunctions, commas, etcetera, as appropriate, the resulting story becomes:

Man (is) Appointed Mortal Sorrow, (but) the Glory of God Shall Descend, Teaching (that) His Death Shall Bring the Despairing Rest (or Comfort).

It's quite remarkable that this first genealogy very closely hits all the high points of the gospel message centuries before Jesus would teach and fulfill the message. It's also fitting that the rest and comfort at the conclusion is accomplished through Noah since he was the only righteous man (Genesis 6:9), provided the redemption for mankind by shielding his family (in the ark) from the judgement of sin (the flood that covered the earth and wiped out most of humankind). In addition, the promised rest is remarkably similar to the rest that Jesus himself promised would come through him:

"Take my yoke upon you and learn from me, for I am gentle and humble in heart, and you will find rest for your souls. For my yoke is easy and my burden is light."

Matthew 11:29-30

The Jewish people have a tradition of reading the Torah, the first five books of our Bible, on a yearly cycle. Each week in synagogue, they read a passage from the Torah. This weekly passage is referred to as a *Parshah*. The first *Parshah*, for example, is *Parshat Bereishit*, which covers from the beginning of Genesis to the story of Noah (Genesis 1:1 – 6:8). They read the last portion of the Torah right before a holiday called Simchat Torah (meaning "Rejoicing in the Law"), which occurs in October, a few weeks after Rosh Hashanah (the Jewish New Year). On Simchat Torah, they read the last portion of the Torah, and proceed immediately to the first paragraph of Genesis, showing that the Torah is a circle, which never ends.

I find it fascinating that their first annual reading, read aloud in synagogues around the world, ends with this genealogy that proclaims the gospel and presents the promise of rest and comfort. It seems unlikely that Jewish rabbis over the centuries intentionally hid the Christian gospel message in their Torah. I contend that it's more likely that this was the divine plan from the beginning.

MEETING JESUS AGAIN FOR THE FIRST TIME

Christianity is centered on the events of that Passover week that lead to the death of Jesus and his subsequent resurrection on that first Easter. It's those events to which all creation pointed from the beginning, and it's the source of our hope. It's the reason John the Baptist so passionately cried. "Look, the *Lamb of God*, who takes away the sin of the world!" (John 1:29, emphasis added). But it's also what we've become so accustomed to that it may even become mundane.

When Alicia and I had just started dating, each time we planned to meet became a special occasion. It didn't really matter how ordinary our plans were, the anticipation often began days in advance. The excitement would build as I would think to myself, "Tomorrow is the day Alicia and I are going to that movie." Then as I woke the next morning, it would change to, "Today!" That entire day would revolve around that evening's event as I would organize my schedule and make sure everything was done so I could get back home with enough time to get ready. Those first months of many relationships are often filled with that same anticipation, because everything is new.

We've now been married fifteen years and, just like any couple that has been together fifteen or more years, there are many adjectives that could probably describe our relationship, but "new" is just not one of them. And that's not a bad thing; it's just different. We now wake up together, go to sleep together, most evenings eat dinner together, and text or call each other multiple times a day, even if it's just to ask if the other needs something at the store, because one of us is stopping. But even with the familiarity that comes with time, we still get those same moments of fresh anticipation we did fifteen years ago.

Alicia and I both travel for work occasionally. With four young kids at home, that means we rarely travel together, since one of us must stay behind to get them off to school and be home when they're done. On a recent week-long trip Alicia made, I was at home with the kids doing the day-to-day tasks. As the time approached for her to return, everyone anticipated her arrival. The kids always asked, "How many days until Mom comes back?" as I put them to bed. Finally, as the evening approached when Alicia was flying back home, the anticipation continued to build. As we texted between her layovers, I found out she wouldn't land until after 10:00 p.m., and by the time she collected her luggage and drove home, it would be close to midnight.

Alicia suggested I just go to bed since she was getting home so late. But, after a week without seeing my wife, I thought, "What's a few extra hours? Wouldn't it be better to stay up and see her when she arrives?" It was that same feeling of anticipation and excitement that I had fifteen years ago, which was being stirred again despite our familiarity. It was almost as if I were meeting Alicia for *the first time all over again.*

Our relationship with the Messiah and Redeemer has some similarities to our personal relationships. There are times of newness, and there are times of familiarity. After long periods of church and life, we sometimes fail to appreciate salvation. We are all familiar with the story of the Passover and the first Easter, but we don't want that familiarity to dilute our passion for them. In essence, we want *to meet Jesus, the Passover Lamb, again for the first time.*

The New Testament has some remarkable stories of how people felt when they met Jesus for the first time. After being called by Jesus, Philip told Nathanael, "We have found the one Moses wrote about in the Law, and about whom the prophets also wrote—Jesus of Nazareth, the son of Joseph" (John 1:45). Nathanael was entirely unimpressed as evidenced by his response, "Nazareth! Can anything good come from there?" But Philip persisted, and, as they approached, Jesus met Nathanael, saying, "Here truly is an Israelite in whom there is no deceit" (John 1:47). The encounter that follows, as Nathanael meets Jesus for the first time, is priceless:

> *"How do you know me?" Nathanael asked. Jesus answered, "I saw you while you were still under the fig tree before Philip called you." Then Nathanael declared, "Rabbi, you are the Son of God; you are the king of Israel." Jesus said, "You believe because I told you I saw you under the fig tree. You will see greater things than that."*
>
> John 1:48-50

Jesus, knowing all that was about to happen, probably had to chuckle to himself at Nathanael's amazement that he could see him under a fig tree. In time, Nathanael, would see the blind given sight, the lame walk, and the dead resurrected. Indeed, Nathanael would "see greater things than that!"

In the chapters to come, we are going to take a fresh look at the connection between Passover and Easter, the reason for the name the "Lamb of God." With fresh eyes, we'll see the significance of the crucifixion occurring in Jerusalem during the Passover festival. And since these events were planned from before creation, we will examine how this was alluded to throughout scripture, from the beginning. It's a beautiful and coherent story that works its way through all history with divine consistency. If you thought the gospel message sewn into the genealogy from Adam to Noah was remarkable, then, in the words of Jesus, "You will see greater things than that." We will see things that were been divinely constructed centuries in advance as we explore God's plan, purpose, and execution of the greatest redemption story that could be imagined.

What Do I Do With It?

As we end, let's return to the verse at the opening of this chapter: "Restore to me the joy of your salvation" (Psalm 51:12a). That's my hope for us as we revisit old stories in the hope of making them new again. To brush off some of the dust of familiarity and to revive our passion. To approach these stories with an open mind and a fresh heart.

I hope that in revisiting the Passover—the story of Easter from the beginning—we can meet the Lamb of God for the first time again and restore the joy of our salvation.

What's in a Name?

- Three -

The First Passover

"I am the Alpha and the Omega," says the Lord God, "who is, and who was, and who is to come, the Almighty."

Revelation 1:8

In the previous chapter, we emphasized that the Lamb of God was "chosen before the creation of the world, but was revealed in these last times for your sake" (1Peter 1:20). Since the name "Lamb of God" and the timing of the crucifixion during the Passover festival invokes thoughts of the Exodus, let's investigate the first Passover and revisit the Exodus with fresh eyes.

The Exodus is one of those great stories that has action, suspense, and drama. It makes for great Sunday school lessons, sermons, and even movies. For those reasons, we are undoubtedly familiar with its elements: the plagues, the Passover, the parting of the sea, and the many other events surrounding the Exodus.

Since the entire epic saga is captivating, the events can sometimes overshadow the purpose and foreshadowing of that first

Passover. Instead of focusing on the story, here we want to specifically investigate God's declared purpose for the Passover and the Exodus that follows, before it happens. Specifically, we'll identify significant details of the first Passover and how they will later connect with the crucifixion.

DOES ORDER MATTER?

Let me start by posing two sequences of events. First, assume the Exodus and Passover were planned first and that Jesus then died in events matching the Passover. Compare that with assuming that Jesus, the Lamb of God, was first planned before creation, followed by the Passover being instated to foreshadow Him. Does the order matter?

There are many situations where the order has a dramatic influence of one's understanding of the situation. Let's take a look at a hypothetical sequence of two events that could occur over two days, with the only thing different being the order. Let's say on the first day I bring my wife flowers, just because I was thinking of her and want to show her my appreciation for all the work she does for our family. Then, on the next day, I do or say something inconsiderate. Now let's swap only the order. What if, on the first day, I do or say something inconsiderate, then follow up the next day with flowers? Does the change in order alter the situation I'm in and her perspective at the end? Probably.

In the first scenario, I contend my wife is grateful for the flowers. Then, however, I follow it up with typical male ignorance, the kind where you say something and then, by the look on your wife's face, you wish you could take it back. After such events, it would be more likely that my wife thinks to herself, "My husband was insensitive, but at least he appreciates me." In the second scenario, however, I'd feel fortunate if the flowers were accepted as a peace offering and go from there.

Likewise, to many of us the order of events are important. If the Passover and Exodus were planned first and served their purpose, then the crucifixion happening during the Passover festival has only marginal significance. However, if indeed the Lamb of God was the original plan from the foundation of the world, and the Passover was instated to point to him, the significance of both are profound.

God spoke to this very idea while Moses was still in Midian, as he was being called to go back to Egypt. God heard the Israelite's groaning, and, while Moses was near Mount Horeb, he saw the burning bush. When Moses saw this "strange sight," he went over to see, and, "God called to him from within the bush, 'Moses! Moses!' And Moses said, 'Here I am'" (Exodus 3:4). After hearing God's plan for rescuing his people, Moses was reluctant and asked God, "If they question me what shall I tell them?" In response, "God said to Moses, 'I AM WHO I AM. This is what you are to say to the Israelites: I AM has sent me to you.'" (Exodus 3:14).

The I AM in Exodus 3:14 is the Hebrew word *hayah*[1] or the verb "to be" or "to exist." It's interesting that when God gave himself a name, it was a verb, rather than a noun like every other name. A verb denotes action. In this case, "to be" as a verb can have three meanings based on the tense. When it's conjugated, "to be," can be read as "I was," as in the past; "I am," as the present; or "I will be," as in the future. I AM includes all three. Here we see, before the Passover and Exodus, God is telling Moses, and us, that I WAS before creation and have had this planned since then, and I AM what you need now, and I WILL BE what you will need, as the redemption story illustrated today will later be completed through the Lamb of God. God is emphasizing that Israel didn't end up in Egypt because the earlier famine was too great. Rather, they needed to be in Egypt so that God could redeem them, in order to set the stage for a final redemption through the Lamb of God. That order makes all the difference.

Look back to the opening verse of this chapter: "'I am the Alpha and the Omega,' says the Lord God, 'who is, and who was, and who is to come, the Almighty'" (Revelation 1:8). Once again, the order does matter, and it's the Lamb of God who came first!

RELIABLE WORDS

Let's take a look at the following words from Isaiah.

> *As the rain and the snow come down from heaven, and do not return to it without watering the earth and making it bud and flourish, so that it yields seed for the sower and bread for the eater, so is my word that goes out from my mouth: It will not return to me empty, but will accomplish what I desire and achieve the purpose for which I sent it.*
>
> Isaiah 55:10-11

What is God saying here? God is emphasizing that when he sends his word with a purpose, the word isn't going to return void. There's power and significance in the word of God, and it's going to accomplish the purposes for which God sent it. Most of us have confidence in this principle; however, many of us can dismiss its significance from time to time. Why is that?

Alicia and I have a long-running internal joke that, "We are the only reliable people we know." Both of us like to take some level of pride in our reliability; that if we say we will do something, we will. Now there's always the situation when the unexpected happens, such as promising to play basketball with my son, but then it rains all day. In those cases, I'd at least acknowledge to him, "I know we planned on basketball, but it's raining today, so let's play tomorrow." But these inevitable changes in plans are not what I'm talking about. More times than I can count, Alicia and I have made arrangements with people to do a job, to attend an event, or to meet us at a specific time. Many times the verbal agreement is face-to-face, less than twenty-four hours before the agreement is to be fulfilled. And yet, so many times as the time comes around, we are left with a no-show and no notice of a cancellation. When they're confronted with the issue, the response is a casual, "Oh, this … came up." Sometimes, it's a good "this," but many times it's not. I'm sure we're not the only people to whom this happens, but it shows a significant trend. People's words are cheap! Often when someone commits to something in words, rather than meaning, "You can count on me," they actually mean: "At this time, it's possible I'll follow through, but don't count on it. If something better, or easier, comes up before then, I'll probably just do that instead, but not tell you." Alicia and I have just learned not to put much trust in promises from people.

Another reason we may not take the words of others seriously, is that we know how often our own commitments are made in haste. Most of us have a cell phone, and at some point, have committed to one of those multiyear contracts that allow us to receive a phone at no cost or at least at a greatly discounted cost. As we sign the contract, there are dozens of boxes signifying agreements to be kept. One of them always states that we agree to pay for all months of the contract, even if the phone is damaged or lost. It's something to which we always agree. But a few months later, when your phone slides out of your pocket and into the driveway just to get backed over, you think to yourself: "I didn't really want to commit to what I signed. I just did it because I thought it would never come up."

This doesn't just happen with "small" promises like cell phone contracts. Every year, millions of people make vows to love each other, "To death do us part," and, "For better or worse." Of course they mean it at the time. I've yet to be at a wedding ceremony and, once the vows are read, have the bride or groom say, "Now that I think about it, I can't commit to that." They're in love, and no couple thinks, at the time, that they will ever break those vows. But it happens. A lot. One reason is that before marriage it's hard to comprehend the significance of what you are vowing.

Many churches have long recognized this challenge and try to prepare couples before they get married. The church where Alicia and I were married was no exception. They required that every couple go through a six-week premarital class before they would agree to perform the ceremony and to let you use the church. In the first class, with eighteen couples, the pastor said that fewer than half the couples would complete the six weeks. I looked around and thought, "No way!" Who would commit to be married and then fail to finish just a six-week class, of which attendance was really the only requirement for passing? But sure enough, six weeks later, there were only five other couples left when we finished.

It doesn't matter if the promises are insignificant or are pivotal, made in haste or well thought-out, people's words are unreliable and fickle. However, God's words are powerful and will achieve their purposes. Period.

THE PURPOSE OF THE PASSOVER

Since the Passover is such a pivotal event in Israel's history and in the foreshadowing of the Lamb of God, let's take a look at what God declares, in his own reliable words, to be his goal and purpose for the Passover.

The events of the Exodus themselves are helpful, and we'll take a look at them later, but since the events are so spectacular, they often over shadow seven short verses, Exodus 6:2-8, where, even before the Passover, God, in great detail, outlines for us his specific purpose, and hence the point of the events to come. Before reading further, I suggest you read through Exodus 6:2-8 and note some of the things God promises, the times he says, "I will," and the verbs he uses. By looking at those elements, one can start to *see* what God has in store through the coming Passover.

Before really digging into these seven verses, let's discuss some elements of what is called rhetorical style. It's well-known to scholars that Hebrew texts are often structured in "parallelisms." These "parallelisms" can take many forms, but one common form is when the stanzas have the pattern ABC-CBA.[2] This form goes by many names and is often called "inverted parallelism," "ring composition," or "chiasm." The mark of such a structure is that the first and last stanzas (A's) have similar elements and form a pair, as do the B's and C's. Bailey points out that one of the highest forms of Hebrew literature is chiasm with seven stanzas,[3] or more specifically, the ABC-D-CBA structure with a fourth stanza, D, in the middle, being the emphasis of the entire writing. He calls this structure the "prophetic rhetorical template." Two of the unique elements of such chiasm are, first, that the main point is in the middle and not at the end and, second, that parallels between the other stanzas often help unlock important meaning. It shouldn't be surprising that when God declares his purpose for the coming Passover and Exodus, he uses this highest form of rhetoric to help guide us in his intentions.

The structure of Exodus 6:2-8 that I propose is outlined in Figure 1 below. Both the introductory (verses 2-5) and closing (verse 8) statements mirror each other and have the same three elements, but with inverted order. The introduction opens with the declaration, "I am the LORD." It then proceeds to recall the patriarchs of the Israelites, Abraham, Isaac, and Jacob, referring to them as "foreigners" in the land. It finishes with God remembering his covenant with them. The closing has each of these three themes, but with different flavors since they are after the work of the Exodus.

It begins with the covenant. But now the covenant is not just remembered, it's *fulfilled*. In particular, the Hebrew word used in verse 8 is *nathan*, which means "granted" or "given as a gift." Next, when Abraham, Isaac, and Jacob are mentioned, they are no longer "foreigners," but they have the land as a possession. Finally, the closing ends, just as the introduction starts, with, "I am the LORD."

The remaining five stanzas are each focused around five specific verbs, or actions of God. In Figure 1, these verbs are underlined, with the Hebrew word italicized, and its translated root meaning provided in parentheses.

A. Introduction:
A1. I am the LORD (verse 2)
A2. Abraham, Isaac, Jacob as foreigners (verses 3-4)
A3. Covenant remembered (verse 5)

   B. I will bring you out from
      under the yoke (*yatsa*, go out, exit) (verse 6)

    C. I will free you (*natsal*, deliver or rescue) (verse 6)

      D. I will redeem you (*ga'al*, to redeem) **with
        outstretched hand** (*natah*, spread out) (verse 6)

    C'. I will take you as my own people
      and I will be your God (*laqach*, receive) (verse 7)

   B'. I will bring you to the land I swore (*bow'*, go in, carry)
      (verse 8)

A'. Closing[4]
A3'. Covenant fulfilled (*nathan*, granted or gifted)   (verse 8)
A2'. Abraham, Isaac, Jacob having a possession (verse 8)
A1'. I am the LORD (verse8)

Figure 1. Rhetorical Structure of Exodus 6:2-8

In the B-B' pair of stanzas, God first promises to bring them out, using the Hebrew word *yatsa* or "go out." This isn't necessarily the leaving of Egypt, but rather, he specifies, "from under the yoke of the Egyptians." That "yoke" was the hard labor under Pharaoh. Think of the bricks without straw.

We can also think of this as an imagery of the "yoke" of sin. In the parallel stanza, B', the verb changes to *bow* or, "go in," or, "carry." Here God specifically contrasts the leaving behind of bondage with the coming into fellowship with him. Specifically, the verb used implies "to carry." That's significant, because God foreshadows that we won't arrive into a final fellowship with him by our own works, but rather by him carrying us into that fellowship.

In the next pair of stanzas, C and C', the actions "to free" and "to receive" are contrasted. In C, it's specifically *natsal* or "to deliver" or "to rescue" that God is promising. This is a complete freedom from the Egyptians, not just their "yoke" as described in the previous stanza. In the parallel stanza, C', the promise is extended not just to freedom from the Egyptians, but the "receiving" of his people. The action "to receive" also emphasizes that God does the work. You can't force someone to receive you; they must do so of their own will.

These parallel stanzas have now setup the climax in the middle. They all point to one primary action of God: the word *ga'al*, or "to redeem." God's purpose in the Passover and in the mighty acts of the Exodus is simply redemption, redemption from bondage and slavery, with a promise of acceptance and rest at the end. This is only the second occurrence of the word *ga'al* up to this point in the Old Testament. Its first use was only a few chapters earlier, at the end of Genesis, when Jacob blesses Joseph's sons saying, "The Angel who has delivered me from all harm—may he bless these boys" (Genesis 48:16). It's fitting that the next time *ga'al* is used is when the descendants of Jacob will be redeemed from their current harm.

This parallel structure highlights something remarkable about this redemption. The acts of redemption that God illustrates here are *transformational*. Looking at the three stanzas before redemption, we see a picture of foreigners in the land, under a burdensome yoke, and of bondage. Yet after this promised redemption, the picture couldn't be more different. The people are received by God, carried by him, and recipients of a gift. Here we see, in God's declared purpose for the Passover, clear ideas of the gospel. Compare these transformational acts of redemption here to Paul's words of, "put off your old self, which is being corrupted by its deceitful desires; to be made new in the attitude of your minds; and to put on the new self, created to be like God in true righteousness and holiness" (Ephesians 4:22-24).

Even before we get to the events of the Passover, we see God, in his own words, layout a purpose that leads to the gospel and to the Lamb of God. Some additional foreshadowing toward the gospel also occurs here as God clarifies "who" does the work. The focus here is always on God, and not us, doing the work. Specifically, each of the five verbs are preceded by, "I will." Furthermore, an important aspect is that it's clearly specified that the fulfillment of the promise is a gift of God.

Another foreshadowing to the gospel is how the redemption is done. In verse 6, redemption comes from an "outstretched" hand. The word God chose to use here is *natah*. *Natah* can have a variety of meanings such as "outstretched" or "uplifted," but it can also mean to "recline" or to "let down." When Abraham's servant is trying to find a bride for Isaac and meets Rebekah at a well, he says, "Please let down your jar that I may have a drink" (Genesis 24:14), where "let down" is the same word, *natah*. Here we have the foreshadowing of redemption coming from God descending to us through Christ Jesus who performs "mighty acts."

Looking at God's stated purpose in the Passover, we see the consistency in his plan. That plan in Exodus 6:2-8 (outlined in Figure 1) starts out with elements of the past, then emphasizes the present redemption, and finishes with the future promise of a completed covenant. Or, as in the words revealed to John, "'The Alpha and the Omega,' says the Lord God, 'who is, and who was, and who is to come'" (Revelation 1:8).

FOUR LAYERS OF REDEMPTION

The Jewish community celebrates the Passover by retelling the story of the Israelites' liberation from slavery in Egypt in a ritual called the Seder. The Seder feast includes readings, drinking wine, telling stories, eating special foods, singing, and other Passover traditions. These traditions are not unlike what we would see in our Thanksgiving traditions. We have traditional foods and reasons why they are served at the Thanksgiving table. Similarly, there are historical stories told that explain of why we celebrate Thanksgiving. Within the Seder there is the *Haggadah* or the "telling," in which stories and readings are done to explain the Passover. The reason behind the "telling" is to fulfill the command, "When your children ask you, 'What does this ceremony mean to you?' then tell them, 'It is the Passover'" (Exodus 12:26-27).

Not unlike our Thanksgiving traditions that have changed over time, the Passover Seder and Haggadah have also been adapted over the centuries. Though there are arguments over what the Passover Seder was like during the life of Jesus, many of the elements preserved in early rabbinic traditions can be traced back to the first century, just after the temple in Jerusalem was destroyed.[5]

One of these elements of the traditional Passover Seder are four cups of wine drunk as part of the Haggadah. Rabbis have connected the meaning of the four cups to the first four verbs[6] in Exodus 6:6-7—the same verbs we just discussed. The Jerusalem Talmud provides an explanation behind the four cups as:

> *Why do we have four cups of wine? R. Yochanan said in the name of Rabbi Benayah, this refers to four stages in the redemption ... "**I will bring you out** from under the burdens of Egypt." Even if He had left us in Egypt to be slaves, He would have ceased the burdensome yoke. For this alone we would have been grateful to Him and therefore we drink the first cup. "**I will deliver you** from their slavery." We drink the cup of salvation for he delivered us completely from serving them. "**I will redeem you** with an outstretched arm ..." we drink the third cup. "**I will take you** ..." The greatest aspect of the redemption is that He brought us near Him and granted us also spiritual redemption. For this we raise the fourth cup. (Emphasis added)[7]*

The four cups are often identified by rabbis as the four layers of redemption. Furthermore, each cup has a traditional name. The first cup is called the "Cup of Sanctification." It symbolizes "I will bring you," where God chose and separated his people. The second cup is called the "Cup of Deliverance." It symbolizes, that we must trust in him for our salvation, and that we are helpless and, "I will deliver you." The third cup is the "Cup of Redemption," marking, "I will redeem you," as salvation requires a price paid with great cost. The fourth cup, the "Cup of Hope or Restoration" is connected to, "I will take you," where God carries us spiritually near to him allowed by the cost paid and is a picture of restoration and completeness.

It's these four cups that Israel has been using for almost two millennia to relive, celebrate, and pass on to their children, God's plan for redemption. If we take the same four elements—

providing freedom, by God's work, at great cost, and bringing us into fellowship—and synthesize them into one sentence, we end up with:

God frees us from the yoke of sin by His effort at great cost to bring us into fellowship with Him.

That's a remarkably good summary of the Christian gospel that the Passover has been pointing to all this time!

What about the fifth verb, "bring you to the land," which we noted in verse 8? The traditional Seder also has a fifth cup, the cup of Elijah, which is poured but not drunk. It's not drunk because they are waiting for Elijah to return. We, however, are waiting for the final layer of redemption: God bringing us to him as the future promise is fulfilled.

DEFINING THE FIRST PASSOVER

Exodus 6:2-8 identified some elements of the coming Passover—freedom (from the yoke of sin) and God's work at great cost—all of which closely match our gospel summary from the previous chapter:

We have all sinned, redemption comes from the death and resurrection of Christ Jesus, it's a gift of God, and accepted through faith.

When comparing the two, we see some remarkable similarities. However, there are also two omissions from Exodus 6:2-8: the requirement of faith and the blood sacrifice. But both of these elements will appear as the Passover is officially defined and carried out.

The story of the Exodus and Passover continue as we read through Exodus. In particular, the ten plagues are outlined in chapters 7-11, culminating in the final plague of the first born (Exodus 11:1-10). In this final plague, we start to see the great cost and foreshadowing of the sacrifice to come as, "Every *firstborn son* in Egypt *will die*, from the *firstborn son* of Pharaoh, who sits on the throne, to the *firstborn son* of the female slave, who is at her hand mill" (Exodus 11:5, emphasis added). After this final plague is announced, we next find the Passover instated and defined.

It's the twelfth chapter of Exodus where the details of the Passover and the foreshadowing of the Lamb of God are outlined. In particular, as we walk through this first Passover, there are four categories that we'll examine: namely, the identified and required sacrifice; the faith needed; the timing; and the communal nature. If it has been a while since you've looked at the Passover story, I recommend taking some time now to reread Exodus 12 and to identify how God's instructions to Moses and Aaron fall into the four categories listed above.

Let's first take a look at the sacrifice. In verse 3, it says, "each man is to take a lamb[8]." It's later clarified that the lambs or goats "must be year-old males without defect" (Exodus 12:5). Why one year-old? Generally, most lambs are slaughtered for meat around six to twelve months of age. Any younger and they haven't added enough weight; but much later than twelve months, and they start adding more fat and toughen up. In essence, these year-old males are expected to be at their highest market value and quality. Furthermore, they must be without defect, so you couldn't sacrifice a poor quality lamb you didn't care to lose.

It's the blood of these perfect lambs that the Israelites were to "put on the sides and tops of their door frames" (Exodus 6:7) as "a sign for you on the houses where you are, and when I see the blood, I will pass over you. No destructive plague will touch you when I strike Egypt" (Exodus 6:13). We see the blood sacrifice introduced: first the blood sacrifice of the perfect Passover lambs, protecting them from destruction and then the Egyptian's first born, allowing the Israelites' release. Here we see the clear imagery: "For Christ, our Passover lamb, has been sacrificed" (1 Corinthians 5:7).

It was the blood of the lambs that could provide redemption and protection only if certain instructions were followed. These instructions were:

> *Put some of the blood on the top and on both sides of the doorframe. None of you shall go out of the door of your house until morning. When the LORD goes through the land to strike down the Egyptians, he will see the blood on the top and sides of the doorframe and will pass over that doorway, and he will not permit the destroyer to enter your houses and strike you down.*
>
> Exodus 12:22-23

In addition to the putting the blood on the doorposts, it was also required that they must remain in the house and entirely consume the roasted lamb (Exodus 12:10). This act required faith in the instructions. The people had to believe in God's instruction and have faith in his words by demonstrating their willingness to remain in their houses. If only the blood was placed on the door posts, the sacrifice could not provide the protection it was intended to achieve. The people must also have faith. The lamb's blood *and* their faith in it were both required for protection from death. Paul emphasizes this same point in Hebrews 11, a section titled "Faith in Action" in some Bibles. Paul explains, "By faith he [Moses] kept the Passover and the application of blood, so that the destroyer of the firstborn would not touch the firstborn of Israel" (Hebrews 11:28).

Through the commissioning of this first Passover, the elements of faith and of a blood sacrifice are invoked. Combining both of these with the earlier elements identified from the sixth chapter of Exodus, we can form a thorough summary of the New Testament gospel to come as, "We have freedom (from the yoke of sin), by faith, in God's work, through a sacrifice, at great cost." All of this is coherently defined and foreshadowed before the Israelites left the bondage of Egypt, millennia before the birth of Jesus.

Timing is critical in all things. Certainly timing is essential when dealing with people and events. We need to be careful when asking for a favor of someone. Catching that other person at the wrong time—for example when their car has just broken down—will probably doom our request. As we continue to compare the Passover to other stories and events, the timing of the Passover will be very important and often will be one of our clues.

In the twelfth chapter of Exodus some key timing indicators are given. In verses 2-3, it is specified that the lambs are to be selected on the tenth day of this first month *(Nisan)*.[9] This first month, called *Nisan* (or *Aviv*) occurs in the spring. We can further identify the timing by the plague of hail where it is noted that, "The flax and barley were destroyed, since the barley had headed and the flax was in bloom" (Exodus 9:31). The Passover, therefore, occurs early in the spring just as barley, one of the first crops, was reaching its time for harvesting.

After the lambs were selected on the tenth day, they were then to be held and inspected until the fourteenth day of the first month (Exodus 12: 6). This waiting period allowed time to verify that the lambs were indeed worthy to be deemed perfect and could be sacrificed. Then, at twilight on the fourteenth day (Exodus 12:6), they would be sacrificed. That evening, they would roast and eat the lamb. The official start of the next day was when the sun went down; therefore, the Passover meal was eaten after twilight, on what was considered the start of the fifteenth day.

The final aspect of the Passover that we want to identify in this inauguration is the required aspects of community and commemoration. God deemed this event so significant in his redemptive plan that it was the first festival defined. He declares, "This is a day you are to commemorate; for the generations to come you shall celebrate it as a festival to the LORD—a lasting ordinance" (Exodus 12:14).

The reason given for the commemoration is that of an instructional aid to all future generations. God wanted the elements that he defined here, and that he used to foreshadow things to come, to be continually taught. It was for, "'When your children ask you, "What does this ceremony mean to you?" then tell them, "It is the Passover sacrifice to the LORD, who passed over the houses of the Israelites in Egypt and spared our homes when he struck down the Egyptians"'" (Exodus 12:26-27). Furthermore, this was to be a community event (Exodus 12:47). A solitary person was not to celebrate the Passover in exclusion. Rather, if any household was too small to completely consume a lamb, they were to share with neighbors.

A remarkable inclusion afforded by the first regulations was that non-Israelites could participate in the Passover, as long as they were permanent members of the community (Exodus 12:42-43). The significance of this is that Gentiles, from the beginning, had always been allowed to participate in redemption, assuming that they demonstrated faith in the God of Israel—faith enough to become a permanent part of the community. Rahab and Ruth are some of these Gentiles of faith, as we'll soon come to see.

This backdrop of community and remembrance form the Seder feast that the Jewish community celebrates to commemorate the Passover. The main three symbolic components of the Seder are specified in Exodus 12:8, as the lamb roasted over the fire, bitter herbs (*maror*), and bread made without yeast (*matzah*). The *Haggadah* (the "telling") within the Seder retells the story of the Exodus for future generations and uses these same elements to tell the story. They use the unleavened bread to explain how, "The dough was without yeast because they had been driven out of Egypt and did not have time to prepare food for themselves." They also ask children the question, "These bitter herbs, which we eat—

what is the reason?" and tell the answer: "Because the Egyptians made the lives of our ancestors bitter in Egypt. As it is said, 'And they made their lives bitter'" (Exodus 1:14).

The Seder has gradually changed over time. Sometimes out of necessity, such as no longer sacrificing a lamb, and instead using a shank bone, since there is no longer a temple to officiate the sacrifice. Other times it has been changed to incorporate additional elements, such as the four cups of wine, to help tell the story. Regardless of the changes and new traditions, the first Passover and the current Seder feast retell God's redemptive plan.

FROM CREATION

We've seen how the Lamb of God, the plan from the beginning, was foreshadowed in the Passover. But it didn't just start there. Again we'll see that these events were setup from the beginning of creation—the actual beginning. That first Passover was so important that God used it to anchor the entire Hebrew calendar. Up to that point, after years in Egypt, it was likely that the Israelites were using the Egyptian calendar. But now they were to be a new nation led by God.

> The LORD said to Moses and Aaron in Egypt, "This month is to be for you the **first month**, the **first month of your year.**
>
> Exodus 12:1-2, emphasis added

God instructed the start of their calendar to be defined by this event and set their new calendar to start in the spring and to begin with the Passover.

In Hebrew there is no specific word for month; rather, it is *chôdesh*, which means the new moon; or, by implication, a month. That's because Israel used a lunar calendar rather than a solar calendar like we do today. A literal reading of the verses above would be this "new moon" is to be for you the first "new moon," the first "new moon" of your year.

If you're not familiar with lunar calendars, the basic idea is that each full cycle of the moon marks a month. Figure 2 shows the phases of the moon that make up the lunar cycle. As you travel clockwise around the circle, the portion of the moon that is illuminated at night by the sun changes shape. It starts with a small

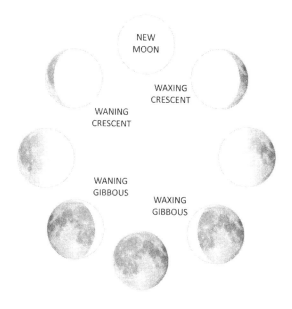

Figure 2. Moon Phases

sliver called a "crescent." Throughout the month, the visible area begins to increase until more than half of the moon appears, which is called a "gibbous." In particular, during the first half of the month, as the visible area increases, the crescent and gibbous are called "waxing." After the cycle is more than half complete, the visible area decreases, leading to a waning gibbous and then a waning crescent. Finally, as the moon is in conjunction with the sun, it is invisible from earth; and then the approximately 29.5-day cycle starts again.

While the night of conjunction is the official new moon, that time cannot be observed. For that reason, the practical new moon, and how it would have been done at the time of Moses, is when it first appears as a slender crescent to the naked eye. Even at the time of the first century, the new moon and the start of the month was still determined by two priests going out at sunset to see if the small sliver of the moon was present. If two priests could observe the small crescent[10], it was declared the new moon. This event was celebrated similar to a Sabbath where, "Also at your times of rejoicing—your appointed festivals and New Moon feasts—you are to sound the trumpets over your burnt offerings" (Numbers 10:10).

We see that the moon was pivotal in marking the months of Israel and therefore the Passover. As we look back to before creation, we see that this wasn't an accident. "And God said, 'Let there be lights in the vault of the sky to separate the day from the night, and let them serve as signs to mark *sacred times*, and days and years'" (Genesis 1:14, emphasis added). These sacred times are called *moed[11]*, or *moedim* in plural. *Moedim* are translated as "appointed times" or "seasons." It was from the beginning of creation that God set the sun and moon in their orbits. The reason, in his own words, was to mark the *moedim*. The entire purpose for the moon was to point to the "appointed times," with Passover being the first festival appointed!

The Passover, inaugurated millennia before the birth of Christ, was meant to point to the gospel he would teach and to the redemption he would bring. It's quite astounding how the details and elements instructed for Moses to follow foreshadowed the Lamb of God. We'll see in the chapters to come that this foreshadowing by God was not limited to just the Passover. Its principles were defined much earlier than the Passover and clarified many times afterwards.

WHAT DO I DO WITH IT?

The Exodus and Passover, at their core, are really just redemption stories that point to the redemption fulfilled at the cross. Yet it's more than just redemption—it's the *purpose* of that redemption. We saw the redemption at the center of the events was to be transformational. It transformed the Israelites from foreigners and slaves who were under a yoke to heirs of a possession marked by freedom. The Exodus illustrates this transformation from a practical situation, and it's the same transformation that Paul emphasizes from a theological perspective, declaring, "So you are no longer a slave, but God's child; and since you are his child, God has made you also an heir" (Galatians 4:7).

As followers of Christ, the transformational nature of redemption is paramount and should permeate our lives. That means it shouldn't be put high on a shelf and taken down only for special occasions. It also can be savored daily in our practical experiences.

Our day-to-day lives are filled with many activities that can tend to overwhelm us with busyness and stress. It's in these times that I remind myself of the transformational redemption, planned from before creation, declared at Passover, and fulfilled through Christ—all as a gift. From that viewpoint, it's hard to take my daily activities too seriously. I find the result is a transformation of my spirit that makes the tasks of the day, the people I encounter, and life in general more enjoyable.

The First Passover

- Four -

Genesis - From the Beginning

These are a shadow of the things that were to come;
the reality, however, is found in Christ.

Colossians 2:17

Through the inauguration of the Passover and the Exodus, we have seen the clear foreshadowing of the Lamb of God and the connection to Easter. If for no other reason, we can see the reasons behind Paul's statement, "For Christ, our Passover lamb, has been sacrificed" (1 Corinthians 5:7). This connection was really the inspiration for this book's title. However, as one of those people who always asks questions, I had to ask the follow up one: "If God so precisely and elegantly defined his redemptive plan in the declaration and instructions of the first Passover, did he start *and* stop there?" There are many well-known prophesies throughout the prophets and Psalms that point to the events of the crucifixion and resurrection; however, that's not what I'm talking about. I'm talking about the Passover. Was it alluded to even before the book of Exodus, and did God provide more insights after it? In this chapter, I want to explore the "before" Exodus half of this question. We'll go back to creation and start working forward to see if the Passover was setup from the beginning.

Moses' response, or lack of response, to God's instructions in the twelfth chapter of Exodus was one of my first clues that the ideas within the Passover were alluded to long ago. The idea of slaughtering a lamb, and spreading its blood around the door as a protection has the potential to sound (and I'll just come out and say it) bizarre! Yet, Moses and the Israelites didn't question, and "did just what the LORD commanded" (Exodus 12:28).

This obedience was prudent and noble, but Moses has a long history of questioning God in far less unusual requests. Think back to the scene of the burning bush. As God told Moses, "I am sending you to bring my people out of Egypt," Moses questions "Who am I that I should go?" Then, after God clarifies, Moses questions again, "What if they don't believe me?", to which God provides Moses with a staff that can be changed to a serpent and provides Moses with the ability to change his hand from clean to leprous and back to clean using his cloak. And yet, even after these signs, Moses still questions God and says "I have never been eloquent," in response to which God provides him his brother Aaron for speaking.

Moses has no problem questioning God when given any instructions with which he was uncomfortable. So, of all the times for Moses to ask, "Really, God?", why not here? It wasn't just Moses, either. It was all the Israelites who obeyed without question (Exodus 12:28), and they too have a long history of complaining and questioning.[1] I contend that the idea of blood sacrifices to provide protection was well-known to the patriarchs and Israelites and therefore was not so unusual from their perspective. This idea must have been foreshadowed long before that first Passover, so let's take a look and see when the shadows of the Passover first begin.

SHADOWS CAST

We are all familiar with how shadows are cast. It takes a good light source, much brighter than the ambient light, shining past an object. As a result, the object blocks a portion of the light, and the object's silhouette appears as a shadow. Shadows of any object can be of different qualities. If the shadow is close to an object, it may have sharp images that are a very good representation of the object. However, as the shadow becomes farther from the original object, the sharpness decreases as the light diffuses. Think of a tree or light post when the sun is low in the horizon as the day ends. The sun's angle produces a long shadow. The shadow near the base is relatively sharp, and the object's original shape can be made out quite easily. But as you look toward the top of the shadow, the edges become faint and the shape stretches, distorting the original object's features. In many cases, long shadows can produce outlines, which, at first glance, don't resemble the original image much at all. Furthermore, if you stand in the shadow at a distance and look toward the light source, it is hard to make out any details. If you begin walking toward the object, the closer you come, the more details you can see.

Another property of a shadow is that, regardless of the quality, it can lead us to the original object. We've all experienced a time when the shadow of some mystery object is cast next to us, but we don't know exactly from what it comes. To find out, you place your hand in the shadow and move it around and can follow the shadow back to its source.

The idea of shadows in the Bible are similar. Paul testifies to the principle of biblical shadows and their role in the Jewish festivals and Sabbath by emphasizing, "These are a shadow of the things that were to come; the reality, however, is found in Christ" (Colossians 2:17). These shadows within scripture follow the same principles as physical shadows. Specifically, that there is a significant light source that shines past an object. The shadow cast by that object projects its shape, and the further away we are from the object, the less defined the images become. But just as with a physical shadow, we can use the silhouette to lead us to the original object, which is the source of the shadow.

To fully understand the shadows that are cast throughout scripture, we have to ask, "What is the most significant element of Christianity?" Without a doubt, the answer is the death, burial, and resurrection of Jesus Christ. Without those events—Jesus' final Passover and the first Easter following it—there is no Christianity. Christ was the point from the beginning. His shadow was cast over the history of creation. The shadow of Christ is there in the law, in the sacrifices, and in the prophets. You can see that they foreshadow him, but they were only the shadow.

When looking at all scripture, in essence, we are looking at the glory of God after the resurrection, shining past the cross, with the cross casting a shadow to the beginning of time. Just as with a physical shadow, the further from the object it is, the fainter the original image becomes. The shadows in Genesis will be the faintest, but as scripture progresses toward the crucifixion, the shadows become sharper and better defined. Finally, as we reach the crucifixion, we stand face-to-face with Jesus. At that point we can see everything in pristine detail: the blood, the tears, and the love. At that point the original image is absolutely clear.

At the Last Supper when Jesus reinterpreted the emblems of Passover, he said, "This cup is a new covenant in my blood which is shed for the remission of sins" (Matthew 26:28). He was signifying to the Disciples, and to us, that in the next few days they would witness the shadows projected into the past now becoming reality. Jesus was emphasizing that the "new" is coming.

The law is only a shadow of the good things that are coming--not the realities themselves. For this reason it can never, by the same sacrifices repeated endlessly year after year, make perfect those who draw near to worship. ... It is impossible for the blood of bulls and goats to take away sins.

Hebrews 10:1, 4[2]

In the old covenant under the law, God commanded them to "obey all these decrees and to fear the LORD our God," with the promise being, "that will be our righteousness" (Deuteronomy 6:24-25). That first covenant was established on man's faithfulness and on his ability to obey. The new covenant is established on God's faithfulness: the work that God has accomplished for us through Jesus Christ. The old covenant failed, not because it wasn't good nor because it didn't declare the truth, but rather it failed because man was weak and did not live by it. The new covenant is established forever, because it is the covenant that is predicated upon God's faithfulness; and surely God is faithful.

Let's now go back to the beginning of creation and look for some of the earliest shadows cast by that first Easter. The outlines may be faint and hard to see, but they will lead us toward Passover and Easter as we follow them to the cross.

ADAM AND EVE

We already have seen, how even the creation of the sun and moon were used to point to the *Moedim*, or sacred times (Genesis 1:14). And we have seen how the genealogy in the fifth chapter of Genesis outlined the gospel message. But now let's take a look at Adam and Eve and see how the shadows of the Passover begin to appear.

The events of "the Fall" are probably some of the most familiar stories in the scripture. We've all heard the story in Sunday school and have likely colored pictures of the "tree" and the "forbidden fruit." It starts with the serpent tempting Eve to eat of the only tree that God forbid them to eat from within the garden. The serpent appeals to Eve's sense of pride and pleasure and convinces her that "surely she wouldn't die" if she disobeyed. It's after Eve succumbs to the temptation and convinces Adam to participate that "the eyes of both of them were opened, and they realized they were naked" (Genesis 3:7). In response to their sin and shame, "they sewed fig leaves together and made *coverings* for themselves" (Genesis 3:7). They knew, without needing to be told, that their sin had to be covered.

Adam and Eve's solution was to fashion garments out of leaves to cover their nakedness. It's important to notice that the garments only covered the nakedness, and must always be worn. Their handmade garments did not resolve their sin. In fact, the word "atonement" in Exodus 30:10, which is used to describe the purpose of many sacrifices, is the Hebrew word *kaphar*[3], which literally means "covering." All the sacrifices of the law and atonement were continually described as just a covering.

God, however, was not satisfied by their man-made "coverings", so he replaced the garments they made by the work of their hands, with garments he had made (Genesis 3:21). In particular, God's better garments were made of animal skins. The shadow of the cross may be faint here, but it's significant that in response to the very first sin, God declares, through action, that sin must be covered and that it can't be covered by man's own work. Rather, God steps in and shows both Adam and Eve that for their sin to be covered, innocent blood must be shed.

Scripture here is silent about what type of animal was slaughtered. All that's said is God "made garments of skin," where the word *owr* ("skin" or "hides") is used. I don't want to make too much of this, but the next two times the word *owr* is used with regard to animal hides, it is for goats and rams.[4] In addition, the next time we hear of an animal sacrifice is when Abel (Genesis 4:4) offers one from his flock, with "flock" most often referring to sheep or goats. This is only my personal opinion, but I think it was very likely that this first blood sacrifice was from a sheep or goat. I find it very provocative that in response to the first sin, it may have been the blood of sheep or goats (the same two animals specified for the first Passover) and that it was the work of God himself, not man.

CAIN AND ABEL

The next sacrificial offerings to be recorded were those of Cain and Abel, the first two sons of Adam and Eve. "We're told that Abel kept flocks, and Cain worked the soil" (Genesis 4:2). The story is rather short on details so we can't say for sure what spurred these offerings to God. Were these regular offerings or was there an occasion that prompted them? We just don't know. However, we do know how these particular offerings went.

We're told that Abel brought "fat portions from some of the firstborn of his flock," and it was this that "The LORD looked with favor on Abel and his offering" (Genesis 4:4). In contrast, Cain "brought some of the fruits of the soil as an offering to the LORD. ... but on Cain and his offering he did not look with favor" (Genesis 4:3,5).

Much has been made about the distinction between these offerings. Many have suggested that God accepted Abel's because he offered a blood sacrifice and that he rejected Cain's, because it was the product of the works of his own hands. Others have suggested that it was not the blood sacrifice that was important; it was that Abel's sacrifice was "fat portions from some of the firstborn of his flock," meaning they were his best. No such distinction was made about Cain's offering. And yet a few have even asked, "How was this even fair—they both tried—why would God reject one gift over the other?"

I believe the real answer lies in Paul's interpretation of the events in the book of Hebrews:

> *By faith Abel brought God a better offering than Cain did. By faith he was commended as righteous, when God spoke well of his offerings. And by faith Abel still speaks, even though he is dead.*

Hebrews 11:4

Why does Paul identify Abel's offering as by faith? I believe within the story it's implied that God had passed on the lesson of the covering of sin through Adam and Eve to their sons. Therefore, Cain and Abel both knew that the acceptable sacrifice, foreshadowing the Lamb of God, had to be a blood sacrifice of the innocent. And, based on Abel's faith, we can see that the prescribed sacrifice, fat portions from the firstborn of the flocks, mirror those of the Passover.

While Abel's offering was based on faith, Cain's offering was rooted in pride. It's not hard to imagine how this situation could arise. The boys were taught what the sacrifice had to be, and it's possible Abel had previously sold his brother offerings from the flock in exchange for fruit from the field. In such a situation there's potential for Cain to tire of this arrangement and question, "Why do I have to continually trade my goods for my brother's flocks just to make an offering?" Almost paralleling his parents, I expect at some point Cain asked, "Did the LORD really say I had to offer a first-born from the flock? Wouldn't my fruit of the field be just as good?" With that thought rooted in pride, we see sin set in motion. The same sin that separated Adam and Eve from the LORD and the garden will now separate Cain from the LORD.

I have always wondered how much God told Adam and Eve about the sacrifice. Were they just told to offer a blood sacrifice from the firstborn of the flock? Or was it a command, like in the inauguration of the Passover where God explained to them that they were to do these sacrifices so that their children will know of redemption? Regardless of the answer, we see that blood sacrifices as an offering were passed down from the beginning. This lesson would have made its way from Adam and Eve, to Noah, to Abraham, to Isaac and Jacob, and eventually to the Israelites and Moses. When we look back to the inauguration of the Passover, it no longer seems unusual that Moses, the man who had no problem asking God, "Why?" didn't blink when God told him to slaughter a one-year-old lamb and to spread the blood across the doorpost for protection. It was something Moses and the Israelites had been taught from the beginning.

ABRAHAM AND ISAAC

As we move toward the first Passover, the faint shadows of the cross that appeared in the opening of Genesis will begin to sharpen. It's in the 22nd chapter of Genesis where we see Abraham tested in the familiar story of God commanding Abraham to sacrifice his son—the son Sarah and he had waited so long to receive.

The typology of Isaac that we see in this chapter is unique in that it's not Isaac's life that provides many of the parallels to Christ, as much as it's that the typology comes into focus through the relationship between Abraham and Isaac. In Abraham and Isaac we are provided a marvelous picture of God the Father and God the Son, with many parallels to the ministry of Christ. Before we take a detailed look at this foreshadowing, I recommend rereading Genesis 22:1-19.

When reading Genesis 22, I see the same care and detail as we found in Exodus 6:2-8, which was investigated last chapter. God here similarly chooses his words precisely, laying a foundation for his redemptive plan. Within this precision, sometimes it's almost as important what isn't said as much as that which is said. As the chapter opens we see such a time as God tells Abraham, "Take your son, your only son" (Genesis 22:2). Was Isaac his only son? Of course not. He had another son named Ishmael, who was thirteen years older than Isaac, through Hagar. But, as God said, "Because it is through Isaac that your offspring will be reckoned" (Genesis 21:12), God did not recognize Abraham's work of the flesh. He only recognized that work of the spirit, the son of promise, Isaac. And this is not the first time God rejected the work of man. The same principle is consistent throughout the Old Testament as God rejected Adam and Eve's covering of sin and as he rejected Cain offering his own work. Just as with the Passover, God unequivocally declares, "You can't redeem yourself, I will redeem you with my mighty acts."

With the command "Take your son, your only son," God also added the description "whom you love" (Genesis 22:2). This is the first occurrence of the word "love" in the Old Testament.[5] Similarly, the first occurrence of "love" in the New Testament[6] occurs in Matthew 3:17: "And a voice from heaven said, 'This is my Son, whom I love; with him I am well pleased.'" The other two Synoptic Gospels also have the first occurrence of love in a likewise manner (Mark 1:11 and Luke 3:22).

It's quite remarkable that the first appearance of love in the Bible is reserved for a father-son relationship rather than man's love for God or the love between a man and a woman. It's here where the love demonstrated on the cross starts casting its shadow into the redemptive plan.

When we look at the Passover-Easter pair and its relationship to the gospel, there are two critical elements: the death, or sacrifice, and the resurrection. The death and sacrifice of the Lamb of God has been present in all the foreshadowing throughout the Bible, but what about the resurrection? In the last chapter we saw the promise of mighty works, for which the resurrection would qualify, but it's not explicitly mentioned. Likewise, the blood sacrifice takes front stage in the stories of Adam and Eve and then of Cain and Abel, but there is no resurrection. Where, up to this point, in the Old Testament, does it speak of the resurrection after three days? We'll see it soon appears through Abraham's faith.

As God continues working in history he said to Abraham, "Go to the region of Moriah. Sacrifice [Isaac] there as a burnt offering on a mountain I will show you." (Genesis 22:2). There is no record of what Abraham thought, only of what he did. He rose early, loaded up his donkey, took Isaac, two servants, and enough wood for the burnt offering and headed out. We know from the rest of the story that Abraham had fully intended to sacrifice Isaac. He showed no hesitation, and if God would have not intervened it would have happened.

It took three days for the group to journey from Beersheba to the mountain God showed Abraham. In Abraham's mind, for those three days he considered his son Isaac as good as dead—because Abraham knew that God had required that he offer him as a sacrifice in the place that God would show him. On the third day the LORD showed Mount Moriah to Abraham; yet Abraham expressed confidence that Isaac would return alive, as demonstrated by his words to his servants "*we* will worship and then *we* will return" (Genesis 22:5, emphasis added). Paul attested to this:

> *By faith Abraham, when God tested him, offered Isaac as a sacrifice. He who had embraced the promises was about to sacrifice his one and only son, even though God had said*

to him, "It is through Isaac that your offspring will be reckoned." Abraham reasoned that God could even raise the dead, and so in a manner of speaking he did receive Isaac back from death.

Hebrews 11:17-19

The foreshadowing of the son as a sacrifice only intensifies as they ascended Mount Moriah. "Abraham took the wood for the burnt offering and placed it on his son Isaac" (Genesis 22:6). It was Isaac who bore the wood for his own sacrifice on his back, just as Jesus bore his own cross on the way to the crucifixion (John 19:17).

It's at this time that Isaac, well taught in the idea of sacrifice, began to ask questions. Isaac asked his father, "The fire and wood are here, but where is the lamb for the burnt offering?" (Genesis 22:7). It's in Abraham's response, through faith, that so much is revealed. Abraham answered, "*God himself will provide* the lamb for the burnt offering my son" (Genesis 22:8, emphasis added). Even at this point, Abraham still intended to sacrifice Isaac and was not expecting a "ram in the thicket." By "*God himself will provide,*" Abraham is saying that, "God provided Isaac to Sarah and I through his own work and not ours. I have faith that God will provide this sacrifice, too." This is such a dramatic change from the previous events where Adam and Eve tried to provide for themselves, then Cain tried, and then Abraham and Sarah tried by using Hagar to provide a son. But here, at the top of Mount Moriah, we see the plan finally comprehended by Abraham. In this event we see the foreshadowing that God himself will provide the sacrifice: Jesus.

Abraham then built the altar, bound his son, and reached out his hand to slay Isaac, when God said, "Do not do anything to him" (Genesis 22:12) and provided a "ram caught by its horns."

Abraham then "went over and took the ram and sacrificed it as a burnt offering instead of his son" (Genesis 22:13).

Here we have another case of what is not said being important. There is no mention of Isaac struggling or resisting being bound by his father. It's not uncommon when seeing artist's renderings of this event or children's lessons to see Isaac portrayed as a small boy. However, it's commonly accepted that Isaac was a teenager or young man when these events occurred.[7] Furthermore, Abraham was well over a hundred years old at the time. It is unlikely that Abraham would have been able to overpower Isaac against his will. The significance of this is that Isaac had to be submissive in order to be bound. We see remarkable similarities here with the predictions in Isaiah:

The LORD has laid on him the iniquity of us all. He was oppressed and afflicted, yet he did not open his mouth; he was led like a lamb to the slaughter, and as a sheep before its shearers is silent, so he did not open his mouth.

Isaiah 53:6-7

This foreshadows the same obedience that Christ demonstrated as he prayed "My Father, if it is possible, may this cup be taken from me. Yet not as I will, but as you will" (Matthew 26:39). I must imagine Isaac asking a similar question as he was being bound, "Father, am I really going to be the sacrificial lamb?" and once being told "Yes," answering in obedience, "As you will."

After these remarkable events, Abraham called that place on Mount Moriah, "The Lord Will Provide." Very significantly, it's noted, "And to this day it is said, 'On the mountain of the LORD it will be provided'" (Genesis 22:14). Mount Moriah is significant for more than just this story. Mount Moriah is also where David purchased Araunah's threshing floor (1 Chronicles 21:18) to build the first holy temple of God, and it's where Solomon completed the temple in 2 Chronicles 3:1.

In Figure 3, the temple area of Jerusalem is shown. The mountains are defined and separated by three valleys. Mount Moriah is in the center and is separated from the Mount of Olives to the east by the Kidron Valley and from Mount Zion on the west by the Tyropoeon Valley. The original City of David makes up the southernmost and lowest portion of Mount Moriah.

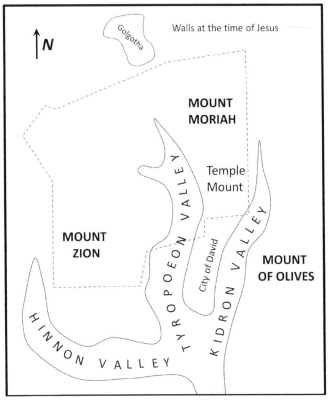

Figure 3. Mountains and Valleys of Jerusalem

Mount Moriah itself consists of three levels. As Abraham approached from the south[8] (Genesis 21:32-34), he would have first come to the lower level, which in about a century would be a Jebusite city. David would later capture this city and make it his

capital. This portion is called the "City of David." Above it, to the
north, is a higher level of Mount Moriah upon which David's son,
Solomon built the temple—called the "temple mount." Where the
temple platform resides, however, is not the highest portion of
Mount Moriah. As you go up further north, the Mount reaches an
even higher elevation. When Abraham and Isaac reached the place
of the Temple Platform, it was likely just a staging point where
they would have prepared for their final ascent to the northern peak
of Moriah, the place where God commanded Abraham to sacrifice
Isaac. The highest peak is called "Golgotha," meaning "the place
of the skull." It was just outside the walls of Jerusalem at the time
of Jesus but was still part of the same Mount that we call the
Temple Mount today. It's at this "high place" on Mount Moriah
that Abraham would have offered up Isaac—the exact same place
about two millennia later that Jesus was crucified.

ABRAHAM, ISAAC, AND REBEKAH

If all we had was the story up to Abraham and Isaac coming down
from Mount Moriah, it alone would still be a remarkable
foreshadowing. We've seen the story of a loved only son, who was
obedient to death, who after three days of being dead to his father,
was restored to life as the LORD provides. However, God
continues the story and out does himself. It's as if he knows that
there will always be those who will doubt and need more. What
comes next is a story that illustrates both remarkable faith, love,
and providence as Isaac is granted a wife.

About three years after Alicia and I married, two of our
friends, Sam and Jenny, were getting married. Sam and I had been
friends since we were 11 years old; Sam had been my best man at
my wedding and now asked me to be his best man. At one point in
the weeks leading up to his wedding, Sam asked me, "How did

you know you were supposed to marry Alicia?" It made me pause. I wouldn't say we had rushed into marriage impulsively, yet I'm not sure I had ever really asked that specific question before I got married.

Part of the reason I feel I had trouble answering that question was that being married, even though it had only been for three years, had changed my perspective. Before being married, I was just a naïve kid who spent his whole life living for himself and who had no clue about what it would be like to be married. I thought I knew what marriage was about, but I really had no idea. So how could I have been sure?

And that was the answer! It was only through providence and the faithfulness of God that Alicia and I found each other and were married. God, in spite of my ignorance, joined us together. It was three years later when confronted with the question, "How did you know?" that I felt truly blessed. If I had been left to "find" my own wife based on my wisdom, it would've been a disaster. The story of Isaac finding his wife is similarly a story of providence, faith, and love, which God uses to foreshadow the next part of the story.

When Abraham was old, he set out to make sure his son Isaac would marry—but not a local Canaanite woman who may have led him astray, but instead a woman from among his own people. Abraham called in his senior servant, Eliezer, and made him swear "by the LORD, the God of heaven, and the God of earth" (Genesis 24:3), that he would find his son a wife from his country and, furthermore, ensure that he wouldn't bring Isaac back there. It was not surprising that since Eliezer had to secure a wife without Isaac being present, he was a little leery. Eliezer asked, "What if the woman is unwilling to come back with me to this land?" (Genesis 24:7). Abraham assured him that in such a case, Eliezer was released from the oath. And with his task assigned,

Eliezer left for the region of Aram and headed to the town of Nahor.

The place Eliezer approached when arriving in the region was a local spring. Immediately upon his arrival he started praying,

> *"May it be that when I say to a young woman, 'Please let down your jar that I may have a drink,' and she says, 'Drink, and I'll water your camels too'—let her be the one you have chosen for your servant Isaac. By this I will know that you have shown kindness to my master."*
>
> *Genesis 24:14*

By God's will, the girl Eliezer met before he finished praying was Rebekah, who was from the house of Abraham's brother. When Rebekah's brother Laban, heard of the events, he said, "This is from the Lord ... take her and go" (Genesis 24:50,51). This was easy for Laban to declare; he didn't have to do anything. Rebekah was the one who had to leave her family and marry a man she had never met, from a lands she didn't know.

It was at this point that something beautiful happened. They asked Rebekah, "Will you go with this man?", and she simply responded, "I will" (Genesis 24:58). The faith demonstrated by Rebekah is astounding, as she agreed to marry a man about whom she knew almost nothing and to go to a place she had never seen. You can imagine how her mind must have been racing on the long journey back to the Negev. This was the most consequential decision she had ever made, and it was done only by faith. When she arrived, Rebekah met her bridegroom for the first time at the well Beer Lahai Roi ("well of the One that sees me"). Rebekah's faith was rewarded as we're told, "So she became his wife, and he loved her" (Genesis 24:67).

The shadow of redemption cast in this story comes from the relationship between Abraham, Isaac, Eliezer, and Rebekah. The name Eliezer means "Comforter," or "The One who helps God."[9] This is the same description of the Holy Spirit listed in the New Testament, where in similar language it reads, "But the *Advocate*, the Holy Spirit, whom the Father will send in my name, will teach you all things and will remind you of everything I have said to you" (John 14:26, emphasis added). Within this story Eliezer represents the Holy Spirit. And the faith Rebekah demonstrates takes on a powerful meaning. Here in this story of Isaac and Rebekah, we see the Father (Abraham) sending his servant (The Holy Spirit) to find a bride, the Church (Rebekah), for his only Son (Isaac), who must accept the offer by faith. The gospel story continues here in remarkable imagery.

The shadows we've seen from the beginning of Genesis through Rebekah have consistent themes. We've seen that the foundation of a blood sacrifice is laid through, Adam and Eve, Cain and Abel, and then Abraham and Isaac. Importantly, in all those stories, it was the work of God that was emphasized and not the work of man. Through Abel, Abraham, Isaac, and Rebekah, faith plays a significant role in those redemption stories. If all we had were the shadows in Genesis, it would have been sufficient to understand the crucifixion during the Passover festival and Easter. It's no wonder that Moses didn't question the idea of a Passover lamb and the protection bestowed from blood on the doorposts. These ideas had been passed down through the generations.

But the shadows didn't stop in Genesis. They continued to be sharpened through the Exodus and the first Passover. We'll see next that the shadows won't end with that first Passover either. God will continue to clarify, with increasing definition, many aspects of Passover and Easter in the events after the Exodus. It will be through Joshua and Ruth that we'll see even more clarity of the Lamb of God to come.

WHAT DO I DO WITH IT?

It's easy to see how the shadows of Easter and the Passover were cast over the events of Genesis and point forward. Once it's viewed as one seamless story, it becomes evident that there is a thread woven through all the stories. That thread is faith. Faith was prominent in Abel's offerings, Abraham and Isaac's obedience, and Rebekah's trust in God.

It's not just the common presence of faith that stands out—it's also the variety of circumstances in which it flourished. Faith flourished in Abel as he offered his sacrifices as prescribed without knowing exactly why it had to be that way. Abraham thought he knew God's plan. He "reasoned that God could even raise the dead" (Hebrews 11:19), so Abraham proceeded to offer Isaac as a sacrifice. However, God had another plan. Isaac had faith in the face of fear. He assumed, not knowing the reason behind his sacrifice, that his father had a purpose, and he trusted him. Finally, Rebekah had faith when facing uncertainty. She had no way of knowing what was to come, but she had faith God would be with her.

That's the power of faith. If we have confidence in God and know there is a purpose in his plans, it doesn't matter if we aren't told why, think we know why but are wrong, or are facing fear or uncertainty. Faith conquers all.

This principle of faith is at odds with our surroundings. We're given basic inspiration to live our lives throughout scripture. We're warned about things to avoid, principles to embrace, and how to treat those around us; yet the world around us tells us they're not important. Rather, we're told to find what seems and feels right in our own eyes (or, more likely, *their* own eyes). That's not what we saw in Abel, Abraham, Isaac, and Rebekah. Despite not knowing and having fear and uncertainty in their particular circumstances, they didn't succumb to what felt right or to what was easy. They all had faith in God having a plan for them.

Five

Joshua and the Passover

*Joshua told the people, "Consecrate yourselves, for
tomorrow the LORD will do amazing things among
you... For the LORD your God dried up the Jordan
before you until you had crossed over. The LORD your
God did to the Jordan what he had done to the Red
Sea when he dried it up before us until we had crossed
over."*

Joshua 3:5, 4:23

We've been tracing the meaning of the Passover and the Lamb of
God through history towards Easter. Before we move to this side
of the Exodus, let's look at the path down which we've gone. The
first step we made was to look at the gospel message. We
summarized, through seven New Testament verses, a concise
summary of the gospel as:

*God **redeems** us, from our sins, through Jesus' **death and
resurrection**, and it's **freely given** to us through faith.*

It's not an exhaustive definition, but it does a nice job at presenting
the main points. It was through this outline of the gospel that we
went back to the inauguration of the Passover, just before the

Exodus, to see how this plan of God was set forth, not on a whim, but from the beginning. Using Exodus 6:2-8, and God's own declared actions, we saw how God outlined his plan and defined the layers of redemption. The summary I proposed from those verses went:

> God *frees* us from the yoke of sin by **His effort** at **great cost** to bring us into fellowship with Him.

Though these statements have different flavors, pairs of ideas emerge. These pairs include redemption and freedom, God's effort and our free gift, and the death and the resurrection with great cost.

Going back further, to the beginning of creation and Genesis, there was ample direction from God pointing to the ideas of a blood sacrifice, his work and not ours, and faith. When put together, there is remarkable continuity, consistency, and I dare say *predictability*, to the entire plan.

A Pivot In Perspective

What we've investigated so far, is, for lack of a better term, the mechanics or formula of redemption. As we move forward, past the events of Passover and Exodus, we're now going to see a pivot in the shadows. A pivot from outlining the *how* of the Lamb of God to the *why* and the *who*.

My family on my father's side are immigrants from the Netherlands. In fact, my father and uncle were both born in the Netherlands and came to the United States at a very young age when my grandparents immigrated to California to start their future as dairy farmers. My grandfather was the oldest of seven children, and eventually, over the next decade, all of his siblings came to Central California. Over time my grandfather bought a dairy in Oregon, and some other siblings moved to parts of

Southern California; however, there is still a large portion of our family who live in close proximity to each other in Central California. Therefore, it's natural for our family reunions to be in Central California. The event lasts four to five days and each day is typically centered around the homes of my dad's cousins, where they take turns hosting meals and events.

The last reunion fell at a time when all four of my kids were still in school for the year, so it wasn't possible for all of us to travel down for the week. Instead, I flew down by myself for a few of the days. As with most family reunions, there was a large and diverse group. There were some grandparents, some babies, and every age in between. A lot of coordination went into organizing the week long meals and events for over one hundred people spanning all age ranges.

One afternoon Alicia called to see how everything was going. I gave her a rundown of all the events, meals, and tours we were doing—essentially the mechanics of the reunion—an outline of the details and the people I met. However, that was not what she was asking. She clarified and said, "I mean, how are the wives doing?" Alicia, as a wife and mother, knew that there was more going on than just the activities and socializing. There were the people behind everything, those who were planning the meals and opening their homes. I wouldn't say that the husbands weren't helping, but we all know they weren't the ones really getting things done. Alicia knew how much work and effort was happening behind the scenes, and she knew that it would be exhausting for them. It was Alicia's perspective that saw the *people* more than the events.

As we move to this side of the Passover, it's that same type of pivot in perspective that we'll make. The mechanics of the Passover and the reasons behind the Lamb of God have been made from a cerebral perspective. Now after that critical image of redemption has been shown, the shadows will shift to the personal aspects of redemption and how the act of redemption will change our fellowship and relationship with God.

From this point forward, we'll use the Passovers that occur in scripture as beacons to guide us through the next shadows. Our next stop will be the book of Joshua. Through Joshua we'll see how the shadow cast by Jesus's crucifixion continues to sharpen. We'll see that both Joshua and Jesus complete the purpose of redemption that was started with the Exodus, and we'll see how their stories provide sharpness and clarity to the outline of redemption we've seen thus far.

JOSHUA AND JESUS

Through the Passover, the Lord redeemed the Israelites and brought them from Egypt, but the story and work didn't end there. As the Israelites left Egypt, they camped at the edge of the desert and were led by a pillar of cloud by day and a pillar of fire by night. They had been freed from Egypt but were still "hemmed in" by the desert on one side and a sea on the other. It was this sea that created a barrier that separated them from a final escape from bondage. From God's outline of the redemption in Exodus 6:2-8 we found that after the transformational act of redemption, were two more promises: the promise of *laqach* or "to receive" us, and finally the promise to *bow* or "carry" us into the final fellowship achieved by his mighty acts of redemption.

It didn't take long for Pharaoh to change his mind regarding the freedom he granted the Israelites. Seeing them hemmed in by the sea, he pursued them. At the sight of Pharaoh's armies marching boldly toward them, the people became terrified. It was a valid fear as they asked themselves, "What good is redemption without the final deliverance?" In response, Moses told the people: "Do not be afraid. Stand firm and you will see the *deliverance* the LORD will bring you today. The Egyptians you see today you will never see again" (Exodus 14:13). It's that word "deliverance," or *yĕshuwah¹* in Hebrew, which will become significant soon. Its root meaning can be either "salvation" or "deliverance" as translated here.

With that promise of deliverance or salvation, Moses stretches out his hand over the sea:

> *And all that night the LORD drove the sea back with a strong east wind and turned it into dry land. The waters were divided, and the Israelites went through the sea on dry ground, with a wall of water on their right and on their left.*
>
> Exodus 14:21-22

The LORD used Moses to part the Red Sea, the final barrier that separated them from freedom, and through these mighty acts they were able to walk into the Sinai desert.

However, through Moses there is an important part missing. The final promise of redemption was the fifth verb, *bow*, "to bring you to the land" (Exodus 6:8). Through Moses this wasn't completed; he just brought them into the desert, not into the Promised Land.

It's near the end of their wandering in the desert that we see Joshua commanded by God to:

> *Be strong and courageous, for you will bring the Israelites into the land I promised them on oath, and I myself will be with you.*
>
> Deuteronomy 31:23

Joshua is the one who would finish the fifth verb of Exodus 6:2-8.

What are some thoughts that come to mind when you think of Joshua? The most well-known story is that of defeating Jericho as God broke down the city walls. To many, the conquest of the Promised Land is the enduring image of Joshua: a view of redemption that emphasizes power. But what about connections with the Passover? These are far less familiar.

The opening of the book of Joshua begins with the announcement of Moses's death (Exodus 1:1). Next the LORD promised to fulfill what he had spoken to Moses and to be with Joshua as He had been with Moses (Exodus 1:3, 5, 17). Joshua is then told to meditate on the law delivered through Moses (Exodus 1:7). With this as the background, it's not surprising that the events of Joshua 1-6 closely parallel Israel's deliverance from Egypt. Since the conquest completes the Exodus, it's fitting the entry into the land is full of Passover-Exodus allusions. It's this connection and the element of deliverance or salvation that will help sharpen the shadows as we come closer to Easter and the Lamb of God.

The first connection between Joshua and the Lamb of God we'll investigate is his name. Joshua is a hybrid of the name of God (YHWH) and *yasha* meaning "to save," "be saved," or "be delivered." Joshua is pronounced in Hebrew as *Yĕhowshuwa* or sometimes contracted to *Yeshua*, and it means "The LORD saves" or the "The LORD is salvation." The name Joshua or *Yĕhowshuwa* is almost identical to *yĕshuwah*, the word Moses used in Exodus 14:13 when the "*deliverance* the LORD will bring" was declared. It's a fitting name for the person God chose to bring his people into the Promised Land and complete the redemption started at the Passover.

There is a saying that, "What everybody knows, no one says." It means that if a group of people are all familiar with an idea or tradition, they don't have to tell each other about it or explicitly explain it to the others. The problem with such a situation is when you're an outsider. Since no one talks about "it," you will never hear about "it" either. I found myself in a similar situation when in a conversation about New Testament names and was told, "You know that Jesus's name was actually Joshua, right?" At the time, I didn't know. They went on to explain, that

Jesus was actually called "Joshua," which in contracted form is *Yeshua*. However, the English translation of the Greek (*Iesous*) translation of the Hebrew (*Yeshua*) name gives us "Jesus." Apparently, it was just one of those things that some people know but don't talk about much. To me, however, it seemed like a big deal, something I couldn't believe people were just keeping to themselves without letting me in on.

I'll admit that just because two people have the same name doesn't mean it's a significant connection. It's fairly common to meet someone with your same first name in the course of daily affairs. However, in this case it's more than just coincidence. When the Son of God, the one through whom salvation would come, had to be named, what name would be appropriate? It seems that Joshua (*Yeshua*), or "The LORD is salvation," would be a good candidate for the one whom John the Baptist would later declare, "Look, the Lamb of God, who takes away the sin of the world!" (John 1:29). And if the Lamb of God was the point from the beginning, it's a fitting name to give Joshua, the one who would complete the deliverance of the Exodus by bringing God's people into the Promised Land.

Here is another example of where the order matters. From my perspective, I don't believe that Joshua was named "The LORD is salvation" first and then Jesus was named after him. Rather, there was no other name fitting the Lamb of God, and his name was always "The LORD is salvation." So it was then Joshua, who was a shadow of Jesus and the salvation to come, who was named after the Lamb of God, to point toward him.

PASSOVER ONCE AGAIN

God had led Joshua and the Israelites right up to the border of the Promised Land at the end of their time in the wilderness. The last barrier they faced was another body of water. This time it was the

Jordan River. As we see from the verses at the opening of this chapter, the events to come will mirror those of the Exodus but this time it's not Moses leading, it's Joshua leading:

So when the people broke camp to cross the Jordan, the priests carrying the ark of the covenant went ahead of them... as soon as the priests who carried the ark reached the Jordan and their feet touched the water's edge, the water from upstream stopped flowing... So the people crossed over opposite Jericho. The priests who carried the ark of the covenant of the LORD stopped in the middle of the Jordan and stood on dry ground, while all Israel passed by until the whole nation had completed the crossing on dry ground.

Joshua 3:14-17

Joshua had finally brought them into the land that was sworn to them. It's just after they enter into the land that we are given a beacon pointing us toward the Passover. We are told, "On the tenth day of the first month the people went up from the Jordan and camped at Gilgal on the eastern border of Jericho" (Joshua 4:19). The tenth day of the first month is the exact same day that the Israelites first selected the lambs in preparation for that first Passover. Then, "On the evening of the fourteenth day of the month, while camped at Gilgal on the plains of Jericho, the Israelites celebrated the Passover" (Joshua 5:10). It's by no accident that the first thing Joshua had the people do once in the Promised Land was to celebrate the Passover.

The details of the events between that tenth and fourteenth days are significant. It had only been forty years since the Israelites had left Egypt by mighty acts and were told to commemorate the Passover "for generations to come." However, shortly after reaching the desert this must have stopped. We know this because, under the Passover restrictions listed, for males to eat the Passover they had to be circumcised.[2] Yet we're told that once in the Promised Land, they had to circumcise all the males born in the wilderness since they had not been circumcised. So at some time between the first few Passovers and now, they had stopped commemorating this remarkable event. It seems that as amazing as those events may have been, the people quickly forgot them.

The next event, which follows the first Passover in the Promised Land, is the familiar fall of Jericho. This was another mighty act of God in his plan of redemption. If we compare the series of events that occurred as the Israelites left Egypt and entered the wilderness with the events that occurred as they left the wilderness and entered the Promised Land, we'll see a remarkable parallel. As they entered the Promised Land, first the barrier (Jordan) was parted, next they celebrated the Passover; and then there was victory through the destruction of Jericho.

Table 2. Comparison of Exodus and Joshua

Exodus	Joshua
1. Destruction of Egypt (First Born)	1. Parting of Barrier (Jordan)
2. Passover	2. Passover
3. Parting of Barrier (Red Sea)	3. Destruction of Jericho

In comparison, when they left Egypt, first there was the destruction of Egypt (the plague of first born), followed by the Passover, and which ended with the parting of a barrier (the Red Sea). The exact same three elements are central, just in reversed order. At the center of each of these monumental sequences is the Passover.

The symbolism here is rich. Why was it that Moses was not able to bring them into the Promised Land?[3] Why was it another, namely Joshua, who would complete the process? It was because there is something more at play here than just the escape from bondage. Immediately prior to the first Passover in the Promised Land, Joshua 5:9 reads" "The LORD said to Joshua, 'Today I have rolled away the *reproach* of Egypt from you.' So the place has been called Gilgal[4] to this day" (emphasis added). The *reproach* mentioned here has its root in the Hebrew *cherpah*[5], meaning shame or disgrace. In this context it's also used to describe taunting or scorn from an enemy. This idea can be seen in the story of Dinah, Jacob's daughter. When Dinah was raped by Shechem and he wanted her as his wife, her brothers responded, "That would be a disgrace to us" (Genesis 34:14). It's *cherpah* that's translated as disgrace in Dinah's situation. But where is the disgrace or scorn from Egypt here? We see that there was more to the story of the Exodus than just the freedom from bondage. There was a layer of redemption that must not have been completed yet, since it wasn't until "today" that the work was completed and that *reproach* was removed.

Identification of this final layer of redemption is best understood by investigating what Moses couldn't do. Moses was considered the representative of the law, since it was through him that God defined the law to the people in the wilderness. However, Moses as the representative of the law, was only able to deliver the Israelites from the bondage of Egypt. He wasn't able to bring them into the land. The land is the visualization of the promised completion of redemption. It represents the final goal: a place where one could take refuge from bondage and achieve what could be described as rest. But the foreshadowing through Moses demonstrates that by mere obedience to the law, simply keeping the law, will never bring you into complete rest. The law cannot bring you into the rest that comes through true fellowship with God!

This picture of slavery and bondage very clearly illustrates what Moses wasn't able to finish. If you are a slave, either literally or figuratively, as in the case of a slave to sin, what seems to be the most important feature at the time is to throw off that bondage and to achieve freedom. However, that's not the end—more is required to finish the process. Any slave that was told "Go, you're free!" would rejoice, but may quickly ask, "What now?" They may have no possessions, no money, no food, and nowhere to go. Is that freedom—to have the yoke removed but be left to die? What's ideally envisioned by anyone enslaved when they imagine freedom is not just the removal of bondage but also the ability to participate in life. They want the ability to provide security for themselves and their families; in essence, the opportunity to fellowship with life. It's that fellowship with life that completes the freedom given. Without it, they'll not be truly free.

The fundamental issue addressed in Joshua, that layer of redemption that "rolls back the reproach," is that in addition to freedom from bondage, or the "go out" of the Exodus, redemption must be completed by being brought into the land. That land is the rest and fellowship with God, the rest in Exodus 6:8 into which he promised to carry them. For us, the bondage is not necessarily slavery to a nation but rather slavery and bondage to sin and the world. We see here that the fundamental issue of redemption isn't the deliverance from sin, the real issue is the entering into the fullness or rest that God has for us. Obviously, redemption is a necessary precursor to that rest, but it's the rest and fellowship that is the final "land" we're brought into.

It's through Joshua (Yeshua) that God foreshadowed the ultimate completion of redemption to come. Moses brought them out of bondage by conquering Egypt. Yet, after the Exodus, Moses (the law) only provided a way to cover their sins. This covering would need to be repeated annually through sacrifices. However, it couldn't completely "roll away the reproach." Once in the Promised Land, another type of bondage would remain: the sin caused by the current inhabitants (Canaanites). This is where the beacon provided by this first Passover in the Promised Land provides a beautiful shadow of the Lamb of God. We are pointed to a more complete deliverance to come through someone who could complete redemption. It's shadowed through Joshua (Yeshua) who brought them into the Promised Land by conquering these potential forces that would separate the people from God. It was through Joshua (Yeshua) that the people were ultimately brought from the law to the Land as the shame or disgrace was rolled away. It's through Joshua (Yeshua) that the people could experience the rest God promised, with no more wandering.

PERFECT REST

Through the story of Joshua, God shows us that the ultimate goal of redemption is not just the deliverance from bondage but also entering into a perfect rest in him. Though Joshua shadowed this rest, neither Moses's nor Joshua's victories provided perfect rest. As the author of Hebrews explains, they were both shadows of the rest to come.

> *For if Joshua had given them rest, God would not have spoken later about another day. There remains, then, a Sabbath-rest for the people of God; for anyone who enters God's rest also rests from their works, just as God did from his.*
>
> Hebrews 4:8-10

It was Jesus (Joshua) as the perfect Passover sacrifice who would completely conquer sin and provided a final redemption.

This promise of perfect rest was a common theme of which Jesus spoke throughout his ministry. He promised, "Come to me, all you who are weary and burdened, and I will give you rest" (Matthew 11:28). He also used Exodus imagery by referring to slavery and the "yoke" of bondage as he continued: "Take my yoke upon you and learn from me, for I am gentle and humble in heart, and you will find rest for your souls. For my yoke is easy and my burden is light" (Matthew 11:29-30). Why is his yoke easy? It's because, as illustrated from the beginning of creation, we don't have to do the work. God promises to do all the work, so our only responsibility is faith.

The perfect rest achieved through the Passover week of Jesus's crucifixion can be identified by comparing that week to the Passovers at the Exodus and Joshua. All three occur at Passover. Similarly, sin and bondage were conquered in all three. In the Exodus and Joshua, final barriers were parted. But in the case of Jesus, which barrier needed parting for us to come into complete rest with God?

While wandering for forty years in the Sinai, the Levitical law was established. It covered many aspects of cleanliness, civil law, annual holidays, and the tabernacle. It's these latter two at which we want to take a quick look. One of the fall feasts is called The Day of Atonement (Yom Kippur), which is still considered to be one of the most holy days in Judaism. We read about this feast in Leviticus 16 and 17. This is the day that the High Priest would carry the blood of a bull and goat through the curtain and into the Most Holy Place in the Tabernacle, the Holy of Holies. The High Priest of the Israelites would then pour the blood onto the altar over the Ark of the Covenant and, in doing so, "Atonement is made once a year for all the sins of the Israelites" (Leviticus 16:34).

This was the only time anyone could enter this area, and God had prescribed a very detailed list of prerequisites for the High

Priest before he could enter. Some of the requirements were the wearing of a sacred tunic (Leviticus 16:4) and offering a bull for his own sin (Leviticus 16:6). There were serious consequences if the rules weren't followed or someone entered on another day. God warned, "He will die" (Leviticus 16:2). The reason was that the LORD himself appeared in the cloud over the atonement cover and for anyone, including the High Priest, to approach it was extraordinary.

The curtain that separated the Holy Place from the Most Holy Place was described in great detail. It was to be made of blue, purple and scarlet yarn and finely twisted linen and hung with gold hooks on four posts of acacia wood, which were overlaid with gold and stood on four silver bases (Exodus 26:31-33). Behind the curtain sat the Ark of the Covenant. Many of the elements and colors were specified because of their symbolic meaning. Specifically, looking at the three colors, blue often represents God's divinity and word[6], purple represents kingship or authority, and scarlet represents blood. All are fitting colors for what this barrier represented.

From its inception, the curtain always separated the people from God and perfect rest in him. However, notice what happens at the crucifixion:

> *And when Jesus had cried out again in a loud voice, he gave up his spirit. At that moment the curtain of the temple was **torn in two** from **top to bottom**. The earth shook, the rocks split.*
>
> Matthew 27:50-51, emphasis added

With his death, Jesus literally and figuratively parted the final barrier separating mankind from God. It was parted from the heavens down to man by the Son of God.

When you look at all three Passovers, it's quite remarkable to see the Exodus (Moses), the Jordan (Joshua), and the crucifixion

(Jesus) side by side. The Red Sea parted after the Passover and Moses showed us the law, but he could not give us rest. The Jordan was parted and Joshua brought the Israelites into the Promised Land after Passover, but he could not give them rest. Finally, Jesus (the new Joshua), was the Passover Lamb and parted the last barrier to rest: the curtain separating us from God. The author of Hebrews outlines the significance well, saying:

> *But when Christ came as high priest of the good things that are now already here, he went through the greater and more perfect tabernacle that is not made with human hands, that is to say, is not a part of this creation. He did not enter by means of the blood of goats and calves; but he entered the Most Holy Place once for all by his own blood, thus obtaining eternal redemption.*

Hebrews 9:11-12

RAHAB

Earlier, when investigating the regulations of the first Passover, we found a remarkable element which afforded non-Israelites or Gentiles the ability to participate in the Passover as long as they were permanent members of the community (Exodus 12:42-43). The significance of this is that Gentiles, from the beginning, had always been allowed to participate in redemption, assuming that they demonstrated faith in the God of Israel—faith enough to become a permanent part of the community. In the Passover sequence of Joshua, we encounter Rahab the prostitute (a Gentile), who, through Passover-like events, would also participate in redemption and ultimately be a recipient of a better redemption.

Before crossing the Jordan, Joshua sent two spies to look over the land, "Especially Jericho" (Joshua 2:1). The two spies ended up in Rahab the prostitute's house, which was built into the walls of Jericho. The king of Jericho quickly heard about the arrival of the spies and their location, so he told Rahab to bring them out. Rahab very shrewdly hid the Israelite spies on her roof under some flax and told the search party that they had left at dusk just before the city gate was closed and that if they hurried they might be able to catch up.

Rahab took a great risk to help a few foreign spies. But she had a good reason. After everybody cleared out, she said to them" "I know that the LORD has given you this land and ... all who live in this country are melting in fear because of you. We have heard how the LORD dried up the water of the Red Sea for you when you came out of Egypt ..." (Joshua 2:9-10). Rahab, the Gentile, had faith that the LORD was going to provide his people with victory, and she wanted no part in standing in the way. In fact, like anyone of faith, she wanted in on the victory.

Rahab continued with her declaration that she knew that the "LORD your God" is the God in heaven and earth. It's a bold claim for someone within the Canaanite region. She ended her plea to the spies saying:

> *Now then, please swear to me by the LORD that you will* **show kindness to my family**, *because* **I have shown kindness to you.** *Give me a sure sign that you will spare the lives of my father and mother, my brothers and sisters, and all who belong to them—and that you will save us from* **death**.

Joshua 2:12-13, emphasis added

The word *kindness* here has richer connotations of faithfulness and love, often used in the context of covenant faithfulness. In the next chapter, another remarkable Gentile woman will demonstrate this same *kindness*. Her actions, near another Passover, will be spoken about in almost the exact same words as Rahab does here, so we'll wait to explore *kindness* more until then.

The request Rahab made was not just "Don't kill me when you come," but more, "Spare us and let us be part of your people." Rahab essentially asked for the LORD to redeem her from sure death.

The spies assured Rahab that if she followed their instructions she would indeed be spared. These instructions mirror those of the Passover. First, she had to tie a scarlet cord to the window that she would lower down to the spies as a sign. Then she would gather her entire family within the house. Anyone who left would die. Finally, she had to remain faithful and not tell anyone of their plan. The Lord allowed Rahab, a Gentile, to participate in a different Passover, and her redemption story began. By faith, she let out a scarlet cord rather than scarlet blood as a sign for death to pass over. By faith, she remained in the house the entire time so she would not perish. Finally, by faith, she was redeemed, as we read, "Joshua spared Rahab the prostitute, with her family and all who belonged to her, because she hid the men Joshua had sent as spies to Jericho—and she lives among the Israelites to this day" (Joshua 6:25).

WHAT DO I DO WITH IT?

One essential element of redemption that we see through Joshua is that the completion of redemption has a consequence. That consequence is that the redeemed "will find rest for your souls" (Matthew 11:29). That rest comes from the Redeemer-Conqueror carrying us into fellowship with Him—the final layer of redemption.

For us, this new arrival into the Promised Land comes with a powerful call. The book of Joshua opens with the Lord telling Joshua to be "strong and courageous" three times in four verses.[7] The reason being: "... for the LORD your God will be with you wherever you go" (Joshua 1:9). Both Joshua and Rahab epitomize this attitude. It's important to clarify that being strong and courageous doesn't means everything will be easy or successful. Once in the Promised Land, the Israelites still had some setbacks and disappointments. Yet, they still had refuge from their previous bondage.

It's important that we don't become fixated solely on the mighty acts that achieved redemption. Yes, they are important, but so is the final goal: rest in the Lord and the fellowship it brings. We can live life with a powerful calling now that redemption is completed. We can live with strength and courage since the Lord is carrying us into the Promised Land.

~ Six ~

Redemption, Rest, and Ruth

Then Naomi said to her two daughters-in-law, "Go back, each of you, to your mother's home. May the LORD show you kindness, as you have shown kindness to your dead husbands and to me. May the LORD grant that each of you will find rest in the home of another husband." Then she kissed them goodbye and they wept aloud.

Ruth 1:8-9

The story of Ruth is one of the most beloved in all the Bible. It's only four chapter long, but tells one of the richest stories, both theologically and dramatically. It starts with tragedy, includes friendship, loyalty, faithfulness, adds a bit of a love story, and ends happily ever after. The book of Ruth takes place during the time of the Judges. While most of Israel is wandering away from God, here we have a story of a Gentile named Ruth whose faith shines with brilliance.

As a quick introduction, Naomi and her husband Elimelek, along with their two sons Mahlon and Kilion, left Bethlehem due to a famine, and headed to Moab on the other side of the Dead Sea.

Upon their arrival in Moab their circumstances quickly degraded. First Elimelek died; then, after Naomi's two sons married Moabite girls, they too both died, leaving only Naomi and her two daughters-in-law, Ruth and Orpah. It's at this point we'll pick up the story, where Naomi has just heard that the LORD came to the aid of his people, so they decide to return to Bethlehem.

Some of the key themes in the book of Ruth are redemption and rest. Both redemption and rest are continuations of themes that occurred in both Joshua and the Exodus and that provide links between these stories. However, those are not the only links. The Passover plays a prominent role in the story of Ruth, although it's never explicitly mentioned.

A unique aspect of the book of Ruth is that the shadow of Easter comes out, not primarily through the events of the story, but rather through the characters of the story. Boaz is a redeeming relative who buys back land that belonged to Elimelek in order to continue the family name. He is a type of Christ; the true redeeming relative. Ruth, the Moabitess, is an image of the Church as the bride of Christ, redeemed by his grace.

We're going to take a look at the story of Ruth through the eyes of the Passover and Easter. From this perspective we'll see the shadows of Easter further sharpened. One of the extraordinary results is that the gospel will reach a new clarity, and we'll see it outlined throughout this story. As we walk through the story of Ruth, let's stay alert to the gospel themes of the need for redemption, redemption achieved through great cost, redemption given as a gift, and redemption accepted by faith. All four can be found in Ruth.

PASSOVER AND RUTH

When I mention Passover and Ruth to people, one of the first questions I often hear is: "There is no Passover in the book of

Ruth. What's the connection?" Indeed, it's true that neither the Passover nor the Exodus are explicitly mentioned in the book of Ruth. Yet the connection between the two are strong.

The first clue occurs when we are told, "So Naomi returned from Moab accompanied by Ruth the Moabite, her daughter-in-law, arriving in Bethlehem as the barley harvest was beginning" (Ruth 1:22). The barley harvest links the events of this story to a specific time in the Jewish calendar. Think back to the inaugural Passover in Exodus 12, where the LORD told Moses, "This month is to be for you the first month, the first month of your year" (Exodus 12:2). That first month was called Aviv or Nisan. This first month, when Passover was to be held, was synced to specific crops. Going back a few weeks before the plague of the first born was the plague of hail. In a subtle footnote we are told: "(The flax and barley were destroyed, since the barley had headed and the flax was in bloom. The wheat and spelt, however, were not destroyed, because they ripen later)" (Exodus 9:31-32). It was the heading of the barley that marked the first month of the Jewish calendar and immediately preceded the Passover.

Passover, therefore, marked the beginning of the barley harvest. Jewish tradition set the practice of selecting the first sheaves of barley the day before Passover, and the bringing of an offering from this early harvest during the festival week[1]. Until this offering was brought, it was forbidden to eat from this new crop. Then for the week of Passover they ate only matzah (made from a portion of last year's crop, which was carefully protected all year from dampness and from contamination by leavening); afterwards they enjoyed the new crop freely, in any form.

Using this information we can pinpoint in time Ruth and Naomi's journey from Moab to Bethlehem. Their journey started in Ruth 1:6, just after they heard that the LORD had provided food to Israel. This information must have come a few weeks before the Passover, when it was clear that the barley harvest was going to be fruitful but was not yet ready. The end of their journey back to Bethlehem is marked by Ruth 1:22, where we're told they arrived "as the barley harvest was beginning." This likely meant a week or two after the Passover celebration, when harvesters would return to the fields. That places the Passover almost exactly during the middle of their journey back to Bethlehem.

Now that we've established that Naomi and Ruth's journey coincided with the time of the Passover, let's look at their path. Figure 4 shows both Moab, their starting point, and Bethlehem, their destination. The shortest path would have been to go north around the Dead Sea and then to cross the Jordan River before arriving in Bethlehem, as shown below.

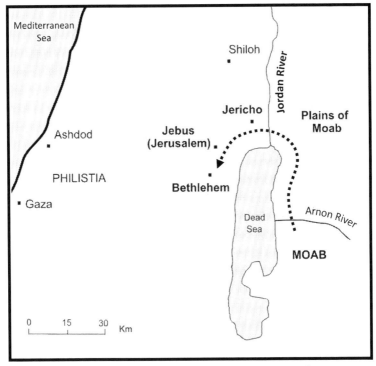

Figure 4. Naomi and Ruth's Path to Bethlehem

This path is remarkably similar to that of the Israelites as they crossed into the Promised Land. They too started in the plains of Moab (Deuteronomy 29:1 and 34:1) before crossing the Jordan across from Jericho and then proceeding to celebrate the first Passover in the Promised Land.

When we connect the timing and the path, we see that Naomi and Ruth arrived at the Jordan River almost exactly at the time of the Passover. They had to cross the Jordan River like Joshua and the Israelites and then proceed to pass Jericho. It may have even been on the Passover when they crossed back into the Promised Land, but we can't say for sure. All we can know is that Naomi would have recognized the Passover was imminent as they were crossing into the Promised Land once again.

The verses at the opening of this chapter highlight some of the personal decisions Naomi and her daughters-in-law had to make. Before leaving for Bethlehem, Naomi pleaded with Ruth and Orpah to stay in Moab with their families. Naomi was convinced they had a better likelihood of securing a "normal" life if they stayed with their own people. It was a very pragmatic view, since what chance would two foreign widows have at forging a good life in a land and culture strange to them?

Orpah agreed and went home, but Ruth resisted. She responded with her own plea:

> *"Don't urge me to leave you or to turn back from you. Where you go I will go, and where you stay I will stay. Your people will be my people and your God my God. Where you die I will die, and there I will be buried. May the LORD deal with me, be it ever so severely, if even death separates you and me."*

Ruth 1:16-17

Naomi, seeing Ruth's mind was set, relented, and she and Ruth proceeded to Bethlehem together.

Where did Ruth's devotion to Naomi and the God of Israel originate? They had been through tough times together and were both widows. I imagine through that adversity they must have formed some strong emotional connections. However, Ruth's words reveal that this connection was more than just with Naomi. She not only showed faithfulness to Naomi but also connected herself to Naomi's people (the Israelites) and to their God. This level of devotion must have come from the stories Ruth heard about Naomi's people and the mighty acts of her God. There was no Bible at this time, nor a written record to which Naomi had access.[2] It was all preserved by oral tradition. Over time, Naomi must have told Ruth all about her God who created the universe, about Abraham and Isaac, Joseph's time in Egypt, how her God had redeemed them with an outstretched arm and parted the Red Sea, and the law that commemorated these events and sets her people apart. It was in these stories that Ruth must have recognized the one true God and began to graft herself into Naomi's people.

This background of Naomi and Ruth is what makes their journey so special. You must expect that Naomi told Ruth, as they were following in the Israelites footsteps and approached the Jordan, "This is the same place in the stories I told you where God led my people through on dry ground into the land he promised to us." Once on the other side, Naomi could point out the twelve stones setup as a memorial of the crossing and recite to Ruth the story, that here: "Joshua set up the twelve stones that had been in the middle of the Jordan at the spot where the priests who carried the ark of the covenant had stood. And they are there to this day" (Joshua 4:9).

Next along their journey to Bethlehem was Jericho. As they passed the broken down walls, Naomi could have said, "Here is where my God broke down the fortified walls and gave us victory." And also, "Ruth, this is the same place Rahab, a Gentile like you helped us defeat Jericho, and she became part of our people!"

This indeed was a special journey for Naomi and Ruth. These two desperate widows, in need of rest and redemption, were walking in the same steps of redemption that brought the Israelites to the Promised Land. Both were able to see, touch, and relive the memorials of past redemption during that Passover. As they walked into Bethlehem just after the Passover, when the barley harvest was starting, they were exhausted and in Naomi's case a little bitter[3], yet they were also spiritually prepared to see how the LORD would once again provide redemption and rest in their lives.

REDEMPTION PERSONALIZED

Scheduling a rendezvous or event requires the intersection of three components. The first two are time and place. If you only agree on the time, everyone will be waiting at the correct time but in different places. Likewise, if the place is agreed on, but not the time, everyone will arrive at different times and never connect. You need both the time and place to intersect. The third component is the people. Just because you know when and where to meet doesn't mean you'll be successful. If you don't know *who* you are meeting, there may be hundreds of people around but you may never connect with the correct person.

When examining the book of Ruth, at this moment in history with Naomi and Ruth, we have the same time as the Passover and the same place as they travel into the Promised Land, but we still need to define the people. The story of Ruth really becomes a story about the people of redemption. In Joshua, we had the Passover, the Jordan, and Joshua as the conqueror. In Exodus we had the Passover, the Red Sea, and Moses as the representative of the law.

In both there was an enemy vanquished, but the final rest that God promised was only partially fulfilled.

This story in Ruth is less about the details of the Passover and covenant and more about the specific action of redemption and what the promised rest of God will look like. In fact, as we already found, the Passover is not even explicitly mentioned. In this story we'll see redemption personalized. Our actors include Boaz, the facilitator of redemption, much like Moses and Joshua were the facilitators of God's mighty acts. Naomi will be the Israelites, who were in the desert but brought into the Promised Land. Ruth is the Gentile participant, who parallels the Gentiles allowed at the first Passover and Rahab, who helped conquer Jericho and became part of Israel. It's through these three people that God further clarifies redemption and rest.

As we continue to approach the crucifixion, the shadow continues to sharpen and imagery starts to focus on the intimate details of the Messiah and redemption. The outline and structure shown in early shadows still exist to form the foundation of Passover and redemption. But now in Ruth, we'll start to be able to make out the outline of the person of the Messiah.

This story takes a different perspective of the Passover than previous events. It doesn't emphasize the power and fear of Joshua or the innocence and guilt of Genesis. Rather, in Ruth we'll see redemption restore honor to those who start in shame.

REDEMPTION SHARPENED

As shadows continue to sharpen, let's look at the characteristics of Ruth as the to-be-redeemed and Boaz as the redeemer. Though Ruth's journey to Bethlehem may have been historically enlightening, she no doubt entered the town with little to no food left and even fewer options, or, as Naomi would say, "empty" (Ruth 1:21).

The first thing Ruth did was to ask Naomi: "Let me go to the fields and pick up the leftover grain behind anyone in whose eyes I find favor" (Ruth 2:2). This process of picking up leftovers from the harvesters was called gleaning. It was a provision God had made for the poor when he commanded, "When you reap the harvest of your land, do not reap to the very edges of your field or gather the gleanings of your harvest.... Leave them for the poor and the foreigner" (Leviticus 19:9-10). It was neither easy nor lucrative, but, if you were poor and had no land, it provided a way to participate in the harvest and gather some food—at least enough to eat for a day or two. And then it *just so happened* that as Ruth went out to scrape together some food for herself and Naomi, she ended up in the field of Boaz, a man who we'll come to see is a near relative of Naomi.

In the events that follow, redemption is sharpened as we explore the characteristics and actions of Ruth as the to-be-redeemed. After gleaning for part of the day, Boaz arrives at his field and notices a new gleaner, Ruth. Once his foreman tells him that she is the Moabite who came back with Naomi, Boaz goes to Ruth and makes an astounding offer. Boaz says to Ruth,

> *"My daughter, listen to me. Don't go and glean in another field and don't go away from here. Stay here with the women who work for me. Watch the field where the men are harvesting, and follow along after the women. I have told the men not to lay a hand on you. And whenever you are thirsty, go and get a drink from the water jars the men have filled."*

> Ruth 2:8-10

Ruth's attitude as the to-be-redeemed, both before and after her encounter with Boaz, is enlightening. She exemplifies and acknowledges the need for unmerited favor (grace). She does this even before gleaning by hoping to "pick up the leftover grain behind anyone in whose eyes I find favor" (Ruth 2: 2). One could imagine that there were those who may take a more entitled attitude than Ruth and say to themselves, "The LORD told the harvesters to leave some behind, so it's my *right* to collect it." Ruth has no such perspective. She acknowledges it's by grace if she collects anything at all. Likewise, even after Boaz extends extra grace to Ruth, she continues to recognize she has no right to his favor, asking, "Why have I found such favor in your eyes that you notice me—a foreigner?" (Ruth 2:10) and further hoping that the "favor" will continue in verse 13.

The gospel idea of redemption, given freely to those through grace, is further expanded by Ruth and Boaz's exchange. A fundamental question that comes in various forms is, "What is the responsibility of the to-be-redeemed?" Since it's a gift, do we get it even when we don't ask? When Boaz answers Ruth about his favor, he responds using phrases such as, "May the Lord repay you for what you have done," and "May you be rewarded" in Ruth 2:11-12. This raises the question: "What work had Ruth done?"

Boaz tells Ruth it's because of what she'd "done for her mother-in-law" (Ruth 2:11). Later in the story, after Ruth declares her desire to carry on Naomi's family name, Boaz says, "This *kindness* is greater than that which you showed earlier" (Ruth 3:10, emphasis added). This is the same *kindness* Naomi[4] acknowledged of Ruth in the verses (Ruth 1:8-9) that opened this chapter. The word translated *kindness* in both cases is the Hebrew word *hesed*[5]. *Hesed* has many dimensions; no single English word captures its meaning completely. *Hesed* spans the ideas of kindness, mercy, selfless love, and faithfulness. It's sometimes even used in the context of faithfulness, as with a covenant.[6] Carolyn Custis James articulates the meaning well:

> *Hesed* is a strong Hebrew word that sums up the ideal lifestyle for God's people. It's the way God intended for

human beings to live together from the beginning—the "love-your-neighbor-as-yourself" brand of living, an active, selfless, sacrificial caring for one another that goes against the grain of our fallen natures.... *Hesed* is driven, not by duty or legal obligation, but by a bone-deep commitment—a loyal, selfless love that motivates a person to do voluntarily what no one has a right to expect or ask of them.... In a nutshell, *hesed* is the gospel lived out.[7]

A close parallel to *hesed* in the New Testament is the Greek word *agapaō* which is also translated as "love." We see it in, "We love because he first loved us" (1 John 4:19). If we mixed the Hebrew and Greek, it would be a fair translation to say, "We *hesed* because he first *hesed* us." When we look at its fundamental meaning, *hesed,* in both Ruth and the gospel is less of a feeling and more about action. One cannot just declare selfless love; it must be demonstrated. It's in the actions of Ruth and Boaz that we get a picture of what this action should look like.

The word *hesed* occurs three times in Ruth: twice by Naomi, describing Ruth and Boaz (Ruth 1:8 and 2:20), and once by Boaz describing Ruth (Ruth 3:10). It's noteworthy that *hesed* is used by both the Israelites who were familiar with God's love and faithfulness, but not by Ruth. Though Ruth doesn't use the specific word *hesed,* she clearly demonstrates it through her actions. By the time we get to the end of the story, although maybe Ruth didn't know how to articulate the specific word, she paints a picture of *hesed* that is recognized by all who are familiar with it.

This *hesed* that Ruth demonstrates is a shadow of the gospel outlined during Jesus' ministry. When asked by a Pharisee, "What is the greatest commandment?", Jesus replied, "'Love the Lord your God with all your heart and with all your soul and with all your mind.' This is the first and greatest commandment. And the second is like it: 'Love your neighbor as yourself.'" (Matthew 22:36-39). These are precisely the two things Ruth did. She first loved the God of Israel and, as a result, demonstrated selfless love to his people.

When examining Ruth and why she found "favor," it's not that she "earned" Boaz's grace, but rather that she chose to participate in *hesed* and as a result was a recipient of *hesed* herself.

Just as Ruth illustrates aspects of redemption through her actions as the to-be-redeemed, Boaz exemplifies the gospel message as the redeemer. When we see Boaz's favor poured out on Ruth, it demonstrates that Boaz recognized his own blessings were from the grace of God. The principle of gleaning that we discussed from Leviticus is also expanded in Deuteronomy. One of the reasons for not picking up scraps of the harvest or going over your field a second time was "so that the LORD your God may bless you in all the work of your hands" (Deuteronomy 24:19). The LORD promises to bless those who allow for the unfortunate.

In addition, the LORD intimately ties together the purpose of gleaning with the Exodus from Egypt and redemption in the same verses. Immediately before and after the instructions to allow for the foreigner, the fatherless, and the widows in Deuteronomy 24:19-21, the LORD says, "Remember that you were slaves in Egypt and the LORD your God redeemed you from there. That is why I command you to do this" (Deuteronomy 24:18). Likewise, here Boaz extended his blessings (*hesed*) to Ruth because God first blessed (*hesed)* him.

The shadow of Boaz as the "redeemer" continues in Ruth 2:14. In a remarkable break in social norms, at meal-time Boaz invited Ruth to sit with the harvesters, and Boaz served Ruth in much the same manner as Jesus served the disciples before Passover (John 13:3-17, Mark 10:31). This was truly a humbling experience as Boaz, a man of standing, stepped out and served the foreign widower—the lowliest person in their culture. There's no way we can know what Boaz was thinking at this moment, but the words of Jesus come to mind: "Jesus replied, 'You do not realize now what I am doing, but later you will understand'" (John 13:70). Boaz may not have known exactly what he was doing at the time, but through his actions he was setting a gospel example of redemption centuries before the true Redeemer would do the same thing.

GRACE AND PEACE

A good synopsis of the gospel can be found by noticing the consistency of the greetings in the epistles of the New Testament. Eighteen of twenty-two New Testament epistles open with the phrase "Grace and peace."[8] A good example is 2 Peter, which opens, "Grace and peace be yours in abundance through the knowledge of God and of Jesus our Lord" (2 Peter 1:2). These themes of grace and peace are exemplified through the interaction of Ruth and Boaz. Upon Ruth acknowledging she needs grace, Boaz met her through action and says, "Grace (I will give you unmerited favor) and peace to you (I will give you comfort and security), I will show you love (*hesed*) because the LORD first loved (*hesed*) me." It's here we see redemption and the gospel take shape well before Jesus's ministry.

This, however, is not the first appearance of the principle of grace and peace. Just after the Exodus, the LORD gave Moses a specific blessing to be used by the priests for all the Israelites. The blessing was, "The LORD bless you and keep you; the LORD make his face shine on you and be *gracious* to you; the LORD turn his face toward you and give you *peace*" (Numbers 6:24-26, emphasis added). This thread of grace and peace runs through the old covenant to the new covenant, going directly through the story of Ruth and Boaz.

REDEMPTION COMPLETED

After Ruth returned from gleaning for the day, Naomi was blown away by her success. There is no way she could have expected Ruth to return with a full ephah of barley, which was equivalent to a half month's wages.[9] When Naomi found out that Ruth gleaned in Boaz's field, she could only attribute the circumstance to *hesed* (Ruth 2:20) and quickly added that Boaz is one of their "kinsman redeemers."

The law of Moses provided for a kinsman redeemer just for the situation in which Naomi and Ruth found themselves. Deuteronomy 25:5-7 explains the details; in essence, if a man died without a son, his widow could not marry just anyone. It was the closest relative's responsibility, likely a brother, to marry the widow, purchase his property (if need be), and produce an offspring. That offspring then would take the name of the deceased, not of the dead brother, for inheritance purposes, thus continuing the family name. It's in this story that Ruth, by providence, wandered into Boaz's field, a kinsman redeemer of theirs, one who could redeem Naomi and Ruth.

Just when you thought the story couldn't get any better, take a look at the genealogy in Matthew 1:5 to see who the mother of Boaz is. It's Rahab![10] The same Rahab who by faith helped Joshua conquer the Promised Land. The same Gentile woman who by faith had to stay in her house to avoid death in order to be redeemed and become part of God's people. It's this same Rahab that Naomi probably told Ruth about only weeks earlier as they passed the rubble of Jericho. And now it's this same Rahab whose descendant will redeem and save another Gentile—this time Ruth.

The word used in Ruth for "kinsman redeemer" is the Hebrew term *ga'al* which is often translated simply "redeem." It's also the same root used for redeem in Exodus 6:7, the central layer of redemption God described before the first Passover. Just in case, you need an extra layer of connection between Ruth, the Passover, redemption, and *hesed*, there is only one other place in scripture where both *ga'al* ("redeemer") and *hesed* appear together. It's in Exodus 15:13, the Song of Moses and Miriam, just after God had redeemed his people by parting the Red Sea with outstretched hand.

It's at this point in the story that Ruth, under the guidance of Naomi, asked Boaz to cover her as a kinsman redeemer. Though Boaz was willing, we find a twist in the story. Boaz replied:

> *"And now it is true that I am a redeemer. Yet there is a redeemer nearer than I. Remain tonight, and in the morning, if he will redeem you, good; let him do it. But if he is not willing to redeem you, then, as the LORD lives, I will redeem you."*

Ruth 3:12-13 ESV

It's through this nearer redeemer that the image of Christ casts another shadow.

To resolve the issue, Boaz immediately went to the town gate, gathered ten elders as witnesses, and met the nearer redeemer. Boaz explained the situation to the unnamed redeemer. He told him of Naomi's return and the piece of land belonging to Elimelek her husband, which needed redeeming.

The unnamed relative initially was willing to redeem the property. But then Boaz added, "On the day you buy the land from Naomi, you also acquire Ruth the Moabite, the dead man's widow, in order to maintain the name of the dead with his property" (Ruth 4:5). Upon finding he'd also need to marry Ruth, the nearer redeemer refused, saying, "You redeem it yourself. I cannot do it" (Ruth 4:6). The reason was, in his own words, that it would "endanger" (Ruth 4:6) his own estate.

Here the nearer redeemer's concern of "endangering" is specifically the word *shachath*[11], which can mean "pollute" or "destroy." It's not that he couldn't; he would just rather not. The significance here is that it's the same word used to describe the plague of the first-born during the inaugural Passover. It was specifically the blood on the sides and top of the doorframe that "will not permit the *destroyer (shachath)* to enter your houses and strike you down" (Exodus 12:23 emphasis added).

The nearer relative is often taken as symbolizing the law. The ten witnesses (Ten Commandments) confirmed his ability to redeem. Significantly, the unnamed man (law) did not fail because of ability, but rather passed responsibility[12]. The shadow provided shows that the Law or old covenant could only condemn—while it is the Passover "sacrifice" that redeems. In this case it was Boaz who, through great cost, would redeem Ruth and Naomi when the rigidity of the law wouldn't. It's through this completion of redemption by Boaz that we see foreshadowing of how the new covenant will interact with the old.

TRUE REST ACHIEVED

After the first Passover, Moses and the law could not provide complete rest. After another Passover, Joshua conquered the Promised Land, but he could not provide complete rest. Here we see that complete rest will come from a redeemer, who through faithfulness and *hesed* will do what the law wouldn't do.

The rest foreshadowed in the story of Ruth is not an absence of work or a state of leisure. Earlier, Naomi prayed for her daughters-in-law: "May the LORD grant that each of you will find rest in the home of another husband" (Ruth 1:9). The life of a wife is many things, but one adjective not often associated with it is "restful." Being a wife includes many responsibilities, and yet that is what Naomi equated with rest. Ruth later spoke of the comfort and ease (Ruth 2:13) that Boaz's favor has given her. In both Naomi's and Ruth's descriptions, it was not a comfort of no labor, but a comfort and rest that comes from security. It's the same rest that the Israelites started to see in the Promised Land, a land that provided security. It's the same security that Jesus spoke of when he said:

> *"Take my yoke upon you and learn from me, for I am gentle and humble in heart, and you will find rest for your souls. For my yoke is easy and my burden is light."*

Matthew 11:29-30

This promised rest is not the absence of trials and persecution, but is a rest that comes from a security guaranteed by the LORD. This is the rest that both Naomi and Ruth are given by the end of the story.

The story of Ruth continues the themes of Joshua. We see once again that the fundamental issue of redemption is the entering into the rest that God has for us—a state of security and spiritual completeness. It was through Joshua (Yeshua) that God foreshadowed the ultimate completion of redemption to come and pointed us to a better deliverance through someone who could complete redemption. It was through Joshua (Yeshua) that the people were ultimately brought from the law to the Promised Land as the shame and disgrace were rolled away. In the book of Ruth, it's now Boaz who sharpened the image of the Lamb of God. He too is a redeemer like Joshua, but he demonstrated a different layer of strength. Not the strength to physically vanquish the Canaanites, but the strength to do at great cost what the law wouldn't do. Boaz pointed to a deliverance to come through someone who could complete redemption once and for all and bring us, like Ruth and Naomi, into the promised rest.

The book of Ruth ends with both Naomi and Ruth redeemed and finding the rest they desired. But it continues to point forward. "So Boaz took Ruth and she became his wife. When he made love to her, the LORD enabled her to conceive, and she gave birth to a son. ... The women living there said, 'Naomi has a son!' And they named him Obed. He was the father of Jesse, the father of David" (Ruth 4:13, 17).

We've taken the story of Passover from creation to the father of David. Next, as we reach the last week of Jesus's earthly ministry, we'll be face-to-face with the Son of David, the Lamb of God, a better redeemer.

WHAT DO I DO WITH IT?

One lesson about redemption we learned from Joshua was that its consequence was rest in the land or, in our case, fellowship with the LORD. That rest is a state of being that is intended to be savored. Within the story of Ruth and Boaz we saw an additional layer of response to redemption: selfless love demonstrated through action—or *hesed*.

The response was the same in both Boaz and Ruth, despite their circumstances being as different as you can imagine. Boaz was a recipient of redemption as part of God's people and was well-off and had resources. Ruth was a foreigner hoping for redemption, who had no resources. Yet they both lived out the *hesed* lifestyle. The lesson is profound. It doesn't matter in what stage of life we are. Whether experiencing success or poverty, joy or sorrow, our response to redemption should be selfless love.

Our motivation behind our actions is sometimes as important as the actions themselves. As an example, recall the lead into the parable of the Good Samaritan.

On one occasion an expert in the law stood up to test Jesus. "Teacher," he asked, "what must I do to inherit eternal life?" ... He answered, " 'Love the Lord your God with all your heart and with all your soul and with all your strength and with all your mind'; and, 'Love your neighbor as yourself.'" ... But he wanted to justify himself, so he asked Jesus, "And who is my neighbor?"

Luke 10:25, 27, 29

In response, Jesus defined "neighbor" through the parable of the Good Samaritan. It's clear that the "expert in the law" was only "loving" to achieve something for himself and hence was trying to define the minimum good he had to do. He had the order all wrong; Boaz and Ruth had the order right. We don't love your neighbor to achieve eternal life. Rather, as a recipient of redemption and as one who could never deserve God's favor, we love because he first loved us.

Let's go ahead and enjoy the fruit of God's mighty acts with outstretched arms. Savor redemption and the rest that it achieves. Then love others, not because we have to, but because it's the natural outpouring of the joy of our salvation.

Seven

Timing of the Last Supper

*Then the Jewish leaders took Jesus from Caiaphas to the
palace of the Roman governor. By now it was early
morning, and to avoid ceremonial uncleanness they did
not enter the palace, because they wanted to be able to eat
the Passover.*

John 18:28

We've followed Passover from the beginning of creation through
the book of Ruth and have seen how the shadow cast by Easter
across the crucifixion has continued to sharpen. As we approach
Passion Week (also known as Holy Week), we'll come face-to-
face with the Passover Lamb and see his image with pristine
clarity. However, before we look in detail at the Passion Week and
its connection to Passover, we need to resolve, or at least discuss,
the timing of events that week.

Passion Week is the time from the traditional Palm Sunday,
when Jesus enters Jerusalem for the Passover festival, through
Easter Sunday. Passion Week is described in Matthew 21-27, Mark
11-15, Luke 19-23, and John chapters 12-19. Also included within
Passion Week are some specific days: Maundy (Holy) Thursday,
the day of the Last Supper, and Good Friday, the day Jesus was
crucified.[1]

Passion Week begins with the Triumphant Entry on Palm Sunday on the back of a colt as prophesied in Zechariah 9:9 and contains several important events: Jesus cleansing the temple (Luke 19:45-46); eating his Last Supper with his disciples in the upper room (Luke 22:7-38); and his going to the garden of Gethsemane to pray as he waited for his hour to come. Finally, Jesus was arrested and taken to several trials before the chief priests, Pontius Pilate, and Herod (Luke 22:54-23:25). Following the trials, Jesus was scourged at the hands of the Roman soldiers, then forced to carry his own cross through the streets of Jerusalem along what is known as the *Via Dolorosa* or "way of sorrows." Jesus was then crucified at Golgotha on the day before the Sabbath, buried, and then gloriously resurrected on Easter Sunday.

The major events of the Passion Week and their order are almost universally agreed upon. However, the specific calendar days on which they occur are not. So why is the specific timing important? One reason the timing is important is that if the Lamb of God was the point from the beginning, and the Passover had been pointing to him all along, we'd expect the events of the Passover and Passion Week to parallel each other. We'll see in the next chapter that they do. However, I'd also say, in many aspects, the specific timing is not that critical after all. But how can it be both?

To answer the previous question, let's recall the Passover chronology from the twelfth chapter of Exodus. It was on the tenth day of Nisan that the lambs were selected then held and inspected until the fourteenth day. On the fourteenth day they were sacrificed before evening. At sundown, which was technically the start of Nisan 15, since the Jewish days were reckoned from sundown to sundown, the lambs were eaten at the Passover meal, which lasted late into the evening.

Therefore, the Lamb of God could fulfill the Passover two ways. First, Jesus could celebrate the Passover meal as the Last

Supper with his disciples on Nisan 14/15, after the lambs were slaughtered, and use the meal to expound on what was to happen the next day. Alternatively, the Last Supper could have been a regular meal before the Passover on Nisan 13/14, and Jesus would have been crucified the next day at the very time the Passover lambs were being slaughtered. Both scenarios result in significant symbolism, just in their own ways. That is why I can simultaneously propose that the timing is important, since it would be enlightening to know which of these two scenarios follows the actual events of the week. Yet at the same time the specific days do not really matter, since either sequence provides significant meaning.

The entire goal of this chapter is to find a specific timeline of the Passion Week for use in the next chapter's discussion. To that end, we'll first explore why there is not a universal consensus regarding the Last Supper occurring on Nisan 13/14 versus Nisan 14/15. Next, I'll outline arguments for and against both timelines and propose which, in my opinion, is the most plausible timeline based on the evidence we have.

With that purpose in mind, I'll suggest that if you're not a details person and have little interest in competing opinions about dates and calendars, go ahead and skip to the last three sections of this chapter if you want. All that's really necessary for the next chapter is for you to understand the timeline we'll assume in the discussion of Passion Week. However, if you find details interesting and want to weigh the evidence for both cases and come to your own conclusion, the following evidence for and against each timeline will be of value. In the end, regardless of if you agree with my conclusion about which timing is correct or not, the chapter that follows will still illustrate the significance of the events of Passion Week.

WHAT'S AGREED UPON

A good place to start in discussing the chronology of the Passion Week is to see where all four Gospels agree. All four Gospels agree that the crucifixion was on a Friday (Matthew 26:20-27:61; Mark 14:17-15:47; Luke 22:14-23:56; John 19:31) and that it occurred during the Passover festival, which included Passover itself and the following Feast of Unleavened Bread. In addition, they also agree these events occurred while Pontius Pilate was procurator of Judea,[2] which can be dated between AD 26 and AD 36. It's this agreement that the crucifixion occurred on a Friday between AD 26 and AD 36 that will help anchor our discussion.

WAS THE LAST SUPPER A PASSOVER MEAL?

Although the Gospels agree on the essential points, many have noted that they appear to differ on which day of the festival was Friday. Namely, was the Last Supper before the Passover i.e. Nisan 13/14 or was it a Passover meal i.e. Nisan 14/15?

According to a straight forward reading of the Synoptic Gospels (Matthew, Mark, and Luke), they all suggest that that Last Supper occurred on Nisan 14/15, "when it was customary to sacrifice the Passover lamb" (Mark 14:12). In John, however, we're told on two occasions that after Jesus's arrest the Passover lambs had yet to be sacrificed (John 18:28 and John 19:14). Upon detailed inspection of John's Gospel, there is no real evidence that John ever maintained the Last Supper was a Passover meal. Therefore, according to the Johannine account, the Last Supper was before the Passover meal, presumably Nisan 13/14.

This debate is not new and can be traced back to the first few centuries of the Church. It even permeates some of our modern religious practices. For example, the Catholic Church and most Protestants use unleavened bread for the Eucharist and

Communion since they view the Last Supper as a Passover meal, which would have used unleavened bread. In contrast, the Greek Orthodox Church and some Eastern churches use leavened bread, which would not be used during a Passover meal.[3]

THREE WAYS OF HARMONIZATION

To many people this apparent uncertainty makes them uncomfortable since logically only one can be correct. For those of us that hold the scriptures as authoritative, there must be an answer. To that end, attempts to harmonize the Gospel accounts have fallen into one of three methods.

1. *Matthew, Mark, and Luke are correct, and John should be interpreted accordingly.* This view is the most traditional and follows the official Catholic Passion Week accounting and the Reformers. Its common appeal is that that since three of the four Gospels agree, only a few words of John need to be "interpreted" or "explained" away to make everything harmonize. However, the three Synoptic Gospels are closely related and don't necessarily constitute a three versus one situation. Rather, it's more consistent to view the comparison as one testimony versus another.

Jeremias[4] provides one of the most complete defenses of the view that the Last Supper was a Passover meal consistent with the synoptic accounts. His argument starts by weighing all the competing viewpoints and ends at an impasse where no conclusive decision can be made, so he claims "the only hope for further progress is some new material." To break the impasse, Jeremias evaluates the characteristics of the Last Supper and finds fourteen characteristics[5] where the Last Supper was consistent with a traditional Passover Seder. However, while well-explained and argued, these similarities, though provocative, are in the end too general to be absolutely conclusive.

2. *John is correct, and Matthew, Mark, and Luke should be interpreted accordingly.* Many have pointed out and suggested that the Last Supper described in all the Gospels does not strictly conform to a Seder format and therefore was not a Passover meal. Rather, Jesus, knowing of his coming arrest, held a meal with his disciples that was Passover-like, but before the Passover, in order to explain and expand on the traditional Jewish Passover.

Arguments made to support such a view note that the most important elements of a Passover meal are either missing or questionable. Neither the eating of a Passover lamb nor bitter herbs, which would be prominent in a Seder, are mentioned in the Gospels. In addition, Mark 14:22 uses the general word for bread, usually referring to leavened bread, rather than unleavened bread, in describing the Last Supper.

Another aspect highlighted to support John's account is that synoptic chronology suffers from the problem that Jesus's trial would have occurred during the feast days following the Passover. This would have been forbidden according to Jewish law, and the Jewish leaders had already expressed a desire to avoid this as they emphasized, "'But not during the festival,' they said, 'or the people may riot.'" (Mark 14:2).

Those who use Jeremias to support the synoptics' chronology often fail to mention that he also raises ten objections[6] to the Last Supper being a Passover meal. Those objections (which include the two listed above) are also explained in detail, and since Jeremias advocates the synoptics' chronology, he provides solutions to each objection. However, as with the fourteen reasons presented to support the Last Supper being a Passover meal, the ten objections to it being a Passover meal, are also too general to be decisive.

3. *Both are correct and can be interpreted as such.* In order for the Last Supper to be both a Passover meal, as viewed by the Synoptic

Gospels, and held before the Passover, as with John, two Passovers had to be held. Advocates of this theory typically cite the diversity of Jewish sects at the time of Jesus. The most prominent factions were the Pharisees, Sadducees, and the Essenes. Disputes over the time to sacrifice the Passover lambs, when to eat the meal, calendars, and possibly the sheer volume of lambs to be slaughtered[7] could have led to the possibility that the Passover was indeed held on multiple days.

One prominent attempt to support this argument was made starting in 1953 by Jaubert.[8] Using ancient texts,[9] she proposed the Essenes used a solar calendar rather than the Jewish lunar calendar. As a result, their feast always fell on the same day of week annually. For the Passover that day, Nisan 14, would have always fallen on a Tuesday, with the sunset beginning Nisan 15 on a Wednesday. Her conclusion is that Jesus must have started the Last Supper on a Tuesday as a Passover meal, according to a different calendar, was arrested on Wednesday, and then the traditional Passover was held on Friday after the crucifixion.

An advantage of this alternative calendar and multiple Passover view is that it solves two problems. The first being that it harmonizes the accounts of all four Gospels. Secondly, it addresses a problem of timing. According to traditional chronology, late at night after the Last Supper, Jesus was arrested and then went through multiple trials before five judges (Ananias, Caiaphas, the Sanhedrin, Pilate, and Herod), all at different locations, before being scourged and later crucified early the next day. That is a remarkably compressed timeline, further made unlikely since Pilate and Herod would have had no reason to accommodate the urgency of the Jewish leaders and, as government officials, would likely, require some time to secure a meeting. However, if Jaubert is correct, her theory allows ample time for the many trials. It's also noted that Mark's Gospel provides some support for this, since it provides details of events for Palm Sunday, the next Monday and Tuesday, but then proceeds to the Last Supper.

Though the multiple calendar theory is compelling, there is no evidence that any Passovers were ever celebrated twice. This would have been a remarkable event, and one would expect that it would've been recorded—yet no record can be found. Both Jeremias and Pope Benedict XVI[10] discuss this theory and conclude that it's fascinating but that is lacks any concrete evidence to be supported.

So what are we to do with these three options? Supporters of each provide "good" reasons why their solution is plausible. Yet skeptics of each provide equally "good" reasons they are not conclusive. Regardless of which one you feel is most compelling, you're in good company. Jeremias (along with many others) is an advocate of (1). Pope Benedict XVI despite Catholic tradition, as well as Klawans,[11] Humphreys and Waddington,[12] and Meier[13] all support (2). Meanwhile, (3), outlined by Jaubert was more recently summarized well and supported by Hahn.[14] My point is that many intelligent and informed people have weighed the evidence and reached different but well-thought out conclusions. I too feel each one is compelling.

However, is that where it must be left? Is there no more evidence to weigh? Before concluding, let's investigate one last piece of evidence.

Astronomical Calculations

We've already discussed that the universal anchor to which all Gospels agree is that the crucifixion occurred on a Friday between AD 26 and AD 36. We also know that Passover was set by a lunar calendar and was in the first month of the year, or spring[15] as set in Exodus. Furthermore, we know how that first month was set by the new moon, as we discussed in Chapter 3. The month started astronomically when the moon was in conjunction with the sun and was invisible from earth. Practically, it started when the first sliver of the moon was visible just after sunset.

With that background, would it be possible to use current astronomical techniques to determine which day of the week the Passover occurred in each of the 11 years between AD 26 and AD 36? The answer is, yes!

The idea of using astronomy to identify when the Passover was during the week of the crucifixion is fairly old. In fact, Jeremias[16], in quite good detail, explains attempts by multiple people in the early nineteenth century[17] to identify the specific day of the week that Passover occurred. Although the moons can be predicted with remarkable accuracy, some sources of uncertainty still exist in determining when the new moon was first visible to the naked eye. Some uncertainties that must be considered when trying to pin point the Passover include: weather (if it was cloudy, one couldn't observe the new moon); the moon's brightness; the moon's visual contrast with the sky; and the moon's position. A full discussion of all these considerations is beyond our scope, but details are provided by both Jeremias[18] and Humphreys and Waddington[19] for those who are interested. What's relevant for us here are their conclusions.

Jeremias, using available astronomical sources at the time, was able to identify that the only years Nisan 14 or 15 fell on a Friday within the years 28 AD to 33 AD[20] were in AD 30 and AD 33 (and remotely possible though unlikely in AD 31). In both those years, Friday was Nisan 14, consistent with John's Gospel. Jeremias concluded that, "It establishes the probability that Friday April 7th, 30 and Friday, April 3, 33 fell on Nisan 14, which would agree with the Johannine chronology[21]." However, due to some disputed calculations at the time, Jeremias found it impossible to absolutely exclude the possibility that Friday in 30 AD was Nisan

15. As a result, he proceeded to rely on the characteristics of the Last Supper to determine which he thought was more probable.

More recently, Humphreys and Waddington[22] revisited the astronomical evidence with increased precision and more observations. Using much the same argument, they arrived at a similar but more decisive conclusion. They found that the only years Nisan 14 or 15 fell on a Friday within the years AD 28 to AD 33 were also AD 30 and AD 33. However, they concluded that on both those years, Friday was *precisely* Nisan 14; therefore, the Last Supper could not have been a Passover meal, so Jesus was crucified at the same time as the Passover lambs. Their conclusion excludes (1) as a possible harmonization and leaves (2) or (3) as the only possibilities.

ASSUMED TIMELINE

With the addition of modern astronomical data, my opinion, is that the most probable answer is that Jesus was crucified on Nisan 14, consistent with John's Gospel. But, I'm not dogmatic about it. Though it seems the most probable, over the last decade I have spent periods of times weighing the evidence differently and leaning toward each view from time-to-time.

The most important point at this juncture is to form a specific chronology of the Passion Week in order to explore the events more closely in the next chapter. By assuming the crucifixion was on Nisan 14, Table 3 below outlines how the specific days of the week match up with the month of Nisan. It can be observed that this chronology is independent of harmonization (2) or (3). Both are the same with the only distinction being if the Last Supper was Thursday or and earlier day.

In the chapter that follows, we'll use Table 3 as our assumed chronology. However, if you feel strongly that the Synoptic Gospel chronology is more probable, the only thing that changes is that the numbers in Table 3 shift to the left, i.e., Sunday is Nisan 10 and Friday is Nisan 15. It's fairly easy to reconcile the next chapter with this modified table by reading only a few phrases differently. If this makes you more comfortable I encourage you to interpret it as such.

Table 3. Passion Week Chronology According to (2,3)

Day	Sun	Mon	Tue	Wed	Thu	Fri	Sat
Nisan	9	10	11	12	13	14	15

Now back to our earlier question: Is it really important to which chronology we prescribe? In one sense, if the crucifixion was indeed at the same time as the Passover lambs, it makes Paul's words, "For Christ, our Passover lamb, has been sacrificed" (1Corinthians 5:7) even more meaningful. Yet if the Last Supper was a Passover meal and Jesus was crucified after the Passover lambs, does that make Jesus' fulfillment of Passover for naught? Of course not! In the same way, Jesus also fulfilled the Day of Atonement, even though he wasn't crucified on that very feast day. Jesus still fulfills both, even though it's impossible he died precisely on both days. So, in that sense, the chronology is not that important after all.

DISPUTABLE MATTERS

In the context of the ground we just covered and the competing viewpoints explored, an excerpt from Romans seems very appropriate:

> *Accept the one whose faith is weak, without quarreling over **disputable matters**. ... One person considers one day more sacred than another; another considers every day*

alike. Each of them should be fully convinced in their own mind.

Romans 14:1, 5 emphasis added

The chronology of the Passion Week is one of those *disputable matters* that people, viewing the same facts but from different perspectives, may still come to a variety of different conclusions. However, this does not distract from what has been called the "Paschal Mystery," a remarkable and life-changing event that may defy absolute comprehension, yet it's glorious none the less.

A fitting summary to this chapter comes from an excerpt from *Jesus of Nazareth: Holy Week From the Entrance Into Jerusalem To The Resurrection:*

> *One thing emerges clearly from the entire tradition: essentially, this farewell meal was not the old Passover, but the new one, which Jesus accomplished in this context. Even though the meal that Jesus shared with the Twelve was not a Passover meal according to the ritual prescriptions of Judaism, nevertheless, in retrospect, the inner connection of the whole event with Jesus' death and Resurrection stood out clearly. It was Jesus' Passover. And in that sense he both did and did not celebrate the Passover: the old rituals could not be carried out – when their time came, Jesus had already died. But he had given himself, and thus he had truly celebrated the Passover with them. The old was not abolished: it was simply brought to its full meaning.*[23]

WHAT DO I DO WITH IT?

There is no shortage of disputable matters that have the potential to cause friction, but it's how we deal with them that's important. Often these matters are minor and based more on personal tradition rather than on essential doctrine. One such example occurred in the early Church. Polycarp of Smyrna knew the disciple John personally, and under his guidance he kept the traditional Jewish Passover on the fourteenth of Nisan. However, Anicetus, the bishop of Rome, tried to force all Christians to fast from Friday to Saturday and to celebrate the Lord's Supper on Sunday. They reached an impasse:

> *For neither could Anicetus persuade Polycarp not to observe what he had always observed with John the disciple of our Lord, and the other apostles with whom he had associated; neither could Polycarp persuade Anicetus to observe it as he said that he ought to follow the customs of the presbyters that had preceded him.*

Ecclesiastical History 5.24.16

But a remarkable thing happened, despite the disagreement:

> *... they communed together, and Anicetus conceded the administration of the eucharist in the church to Polycarp, manifestly as a mark of respect. And they parted from each other in peace, both those who observed, and those who did not, maintaining the peace of the whole church.*

Ecclesiastical History 5.24.17

In the face of disputable matters, they communed, offered each other respect, and lived in peace.

The lesson is clear. As Christians, we agree on the essential elements—the completion of redemption brought by the death and resurrection of Christ. We can dispute the small things, such as what to wear to Church, music, whether to have grape juice or wine for communion, and a myriad of others things—but, despite those disputable matters, we should still commune with love and peace.

Timing of the Last Supper

- Eight -

Face to Face with the Lamb of God

*When he came near the place where the road goes down
the Mount of Olives, the whole crowd of disciples began
joyfully to praise God in loud voices for all the miracles
they had seen: "Blessed is the king who comes in the name
of the Lord!" "Peace in heaven and glory in the highest!"*

Luke 19:37-38

As the opening verses highlight, we have reached the culminating
week in Jesus's ministry, to which all the prior Passovers have
pointed. The Passion Week was not the first Passover the Gospels
record, yet this one is the climax. We've followed the shadow of
this Passover from the beginning. We saw the precedence for
blood sacrifices early on. It led us to God's declaration of the
Passover's purpose in Exodus 6:2-8. Later, as we continued
walking toward the crucifixion we saw the meaning of redemption
expanded through Joshua. Even further down this path, it was
through Ruth and Boaz that the redeemed and the redeemer were
personalized, as both rest and redemption came further into focus.

We started following faint shadows with edges that only remotely matched its source. Yet as we walked closer to the Lamb of God, his image became sharper. Now, as we walk with Jesus as he makes his way to Jerusalem for the last time, we'll find ourselves looking face-to-face with the Lamb of God. We'll be so close that we'll no longer be looking at his shadow but *directly* at him. We'll be close enough that we can see the features of his face, the blood from his wounds, his tears, and even his grace as he tells one of those being crucified next to him, "Truly I tell you, today you will be with me in paradise" (Luke 23:43).

HISTORIC EVENTS

Children have great imaginations. They approach the world with hope and fervor and still consider all things possible. As children we all played those games where we would pose hypothetical and imaginary questions such as, "If you were invisible, what would you do?" or, "If you could meet anybody from history, who would it be?" Unfortunately, as adults we rarely allow ourselves time to splurge on such impractical lines of questioning. However, there has been one such question that, even as an adult, I still indulge: "If I could go back and witness any biblical event and experience it in person, which events would rank the highest?"

That question has led me over the years to keep a "mental" top ten list of events. Many are obvious choices, such as the parting of the Red Sea. It would be amazing to go back and witness first-hand this mighty act of God and walk through on dry ground with the Israelites as they escaped Pharaoh. Another event near the top of my list is Elijah's throw down with the prophets of Baal on Mount Carmel. The way he mock's the false prophets and then calls down fire from heaven makes for great theater.

Other events on my list, however, may not be on most people's lists. Two that make my top ten list bookend the Passion

Week and the culminating Passover. The first is the Triumphant Entry that opened this chapter. Knowing what I know now, and looking back at this event through the lens of history, makes Jesus's arrival in Jerusalem have the utmost significance. The people spontaneously gathered to praise Jesus, the Lamb of God, as he rode up to Jerusalem to fulfill his destiny. They may not have fully comprehended the magnitude of what they were doing, yet they felt compelled to do it. The opportunity to participate alongside them in this historic hour is almost too much for me to fathom. And, as we'll soon see there is a lot of significance to this event.

The other event that makes my list is an often overlooked meeting just after the resurrection. Two of Jesus's followers were walking to Emmaus when Jesus asked them what they were discussing. As we're then told, "Beginning with Moses and all the Prophets, he explained to them what was said in *all* the Scriptures concerning himself" (Luke 24:27, emphasis added). How great would that be to just sit in on that lesson! In Jesus's own words, starting from Moses, *all* that the scriptures said about him. The same story of Passover from the beginning that we've traced, but with absolute authority and no speculation. It just blows my mind.

Using the Triumphant Entry and road to Emmaus as context, let's explore the details of the Passion Week with fresh eyes. By that I mean let's not just look at the events as far away history, but let's imagine ourselves in these experiences. Let's walk side by side with the Disciples and with Jesus in these final few hours of Jesus's earthly life.

THE PASSOVER LAMBS GATHER

The Passover, followed by the week-long Feast of Unleavened Bread, were the first feasts of the Jewish year and one of the three pilgrimage feasts. As a result, the population of Jerusalem would swell as the Passover approached. It marked a very specific purpose as a memorial of redemption. This redemption was by the blood sacrifice of a lamb without defect, which according to the twelfth chapter of Exodus, was brought in on the tenth day of Nisan, inspected until the fourteenth of Nisan, and then sacrificed at twilight.

Accounts of the population of Jerusalem during the Passover at the time of Jesus vary widely. However, a good median estimate suggests 100,000 to 200,000 people were present, including festival visitors.[1] To accommodate that many people celebrating a Passover meal, it would likely take more than 10,000 lambs. Arranging for that many lambs to arrive at Jerusalem by Nisan 10 and to be monitored until Nisan 14 must have been quite a task. It would require the nearby flocks to begin being shepherded toward the city well in advance of the tenth. It's at this same time that Jesus set out toward Jerusalem from Bethany, approaching Jerusalem as the Lamb of God at the same time as tens of thousands of Passover lambs were making the same trip.

THE TRIUMPHANT ENTRY

As he approached the Mount of Olives, Jesus, only a few miles by foot from Jerusalem, sent two disciples ahead to find a colt no one had ever ridden. This was going to be his ride into Jerusalem as was predicted centuries ago (Zechariah 9:9). According to our earlier calendar in Table 3, this Sunday, known as Palm Sunday, was Nisan 9. Jesus was approaching Jerusalem at the same time all the Passover lambs were gathering outside the city in preparation for their four-day-long inspection.

Just as Jesus, riding on the colt, came to the point in the road where it begins to descend, people began to gather and lay their cloaks on the road. The spontaneous outpouring of the people that followed is described as:

> ... the great crowd that had come for the festival heard that Jesus was on his way to Jerusalem. They took palm branches and went out to meet him, shouting, "Hosanna!" "Blessed is he who comes in the name of the Lord!" "Blessed is the king of Israel!"
>
> John 12:12-13

The specific words chosen by the people are significant. The word *Hosanna* is a Hebrew expression meaning "save," which was also used an exclamation of praise. Recall earlier where we discussed how Jesus's name, also Joshua or Yeshua, means "The LORD is salvation," or "LORD, save us." So just imagine yourself on the road-side to Jerusalem with thousands of people waving palm branches. Just as all the Passover lambs are being gathered around Jerusalem, the people are yelling, "Save us!" to Jesus, whose name literally means "LORD, save us" as he rides up to the gates of Jerusalem.

We can have confidence this was all a spontaneous outpouring of the people, since we're told, "At first his *disciples did not understand all this.* Only after Jesus was glorified did they realize that these things had been written about him and that these things had been done to him" (John 12:16, emphasis added). The Disciples had no idea they were going to be met with such an event and, at that moment, couldn't even see the significance.

It's not just the single word *Hosanna* that is significant. In all four Gospels the phrase, "Blessed is he who comes in the name of the Lord!" is used. It comes from Psalm 118, a Messianic Psalm which is part of the Hallel. The Hallel consists of six Psalms (113–118), which are recited as a unit, on joyous occasions including the three pilgrim festivals, of which Passover is one. It's these same

Psalms that also are traditionally cited at different times throughout the Passover Seder. An excerpt from Psalm 118 from which the words of the Triumphant Entry originate is:

> *I will praise You, For You have answered me, And have become my salvation. The stone which the builders rejected Has become the chief cornerstone. This was the LORD's doing; It is marvelous in our eyes.* **This is the day the LORD has made; We will rejoice and be glad in it.** *Save now, I pray, O LORD; O LORD, I pray, send now prosperity. Blessed is he who comes in the name of the LORD! We have blessed you from the house of the LORD.*
>
> Psalm 118:21-26, NKJV emphasis added

Within this Psalm many may recognize the inspiration for a familiar hymn, "This is the Day."[2] Often we take this Psalm to mean, "Rejoice in a day, because the Lord made it." Of course that's a solid principle, and I encourage you to rejoice in every day. However, that's not what is spoken of here. This Psalm is talking about *this* day. It's a Messianic Psalm that points to *this* very day in history when Jesus, the Passover Lamb, who was established before creation, would be presented to Jerusalem.

It was tragic how the Pharisees responded to *this* day: "Some of the Pharisees in the crowd said to Jesus, 'Teacher, rebuke your disciples!'" (Luke 19:39). Although the Disciples didn't fully grasp what was happening, the Pharisees did see the significance; yet they still had hardened hearts. Jesus responded to their complaint by saying, "'I tell you,' he replied, 'if they keep quiet, the stones will cry out'" (Luke 19:40). I'm not sure if Jesus was using hyperbole or not in this situation. All creation had been working toward *this* day, and creation may indeed have not stood silent for *this* day if the Pharisees subdued the crowds.

The Lamb of God Inspected

The next element in the chronology of any Passover, once the lambs arrived, was their inspection from the tenth to fourteenth days of the month. This is exactly what happened with Jesus. During that period, we often look at the details of Jesus's teaching, his interaction with the Jewish leaders, and his arrest. In effect, we focus on the individual events that make up those days. However, if we take a high-level perspective, those events are all just inspections of the Lamb of God.

The teachers of the law, spent most of the time during those days attempting to trap Jesus. "Keeping a close watch on him, they sent spies, who pretended to be sincere. They hoped to catch Jesus in something he said, so that they might hand him over to the power and authority of the governor" (Luke 20:20). One of their tests came as the following question: "Is it right for us to pay taxes to Caesar or not?" (Luke 20:22). Seeing through their trap Jesus addressed them:

> *"Show me a denarius. Whose image and inscription are on it?" "Caesar's," they replied. He said to them, "Then give back to Caesar what is Caesar's, and to God what is God's." They were unable to trap him in what he had said there in public. And astonished by his answer, they became silent.*
>
> Luke 20:24-26

They were not able to find defect in the Lamb of God! This process continued over the next days, always with the same result.

Near the end of this inspection period, the Last Supper occurred. According to our chronology, this would have been at the end of Nisan 13 and the start of Nisan 14, as the sun went down (or possibly a day earlier.) Judas left that evening to put in motion Jesus's arrest in a few hours. After Jesus was arrested late that evening, his final inspection began. From the time of his arrest to the crucifixion, Jesus would be tried before five different judges (Ananias, Caiaphas, the Sanhedrin, Pilate, and Herod) and would have six trials (two by Pilate.)

Table 4. Trials of Jesus

Trial	References
1. Before Annas.	John 18:12-14,19-23
2. Before Caiaphas and Sanhedrin at Caiaphas' house.	Matthew 26:57-61
3. Before Caiaphas and Sanhedrin in the Hall of Hewn Stone, the meeting place of the Sanhedrin.	Matthew 27:1, Luke 22:66-71
4. Before Pilate (the first time).	Luke 23:1-5, Matthew 27:2,11-14, Mark 15:1-5, John 18:28-28
5. Before Herod.	Luke 23:6-11
6. Before Pilate (the second time).	Luke 23:13-15

All these trials have a similar flavor. First, charges are brought forward, then the "judge" declares a verdict. In the case of the first trial with Pilate, "...they began to accuse him, saying, 'We have found this man subverting our nation. He opposes payment of taxes to Caesar and claims to be Messiah, a king.'" (Luke 23:2). After Pilate investigated the matter, he declared, "I find no basis for a charge against this man" (Luke 23:4). Likewise, after being sent to Herod and returning a second time to Pilate, it was declared:

> *"You brought me this man as one who was inciting the people to rebellion. I have examined him in your presence and have found no basis for your charges against him. Neither has Herod, for he sent him back to us; as you can see, he has done nothing to deserve death."*
>
> Luke 23:14-15

Every time the verdict is the same: The Lamb of God is without defect. It's ironic that the people who were trying to accuse Jesus and were fearful of him, were the same ones who in a sense made provision for him to be declared *worthy* of the distinction of being the Lamb of God.

WAS THERE ANY OTHER WAY?

For a moment let's return to a question posed at the start of our investigation and asked by many at one time or another: "Did it have to be this way?" Did Jesus, the Son of God, have to be perfect and be sacrificed as the Lamb of God to provide redemption? For those of us who were raised within a Christian sphere of influence, you almost feel guilty even thinking such a question, since we know the answer. However, for skeptics, it's a natural and fair question. It's comforting to me that Jesus himself asks this very same question. He prays just before his arrest, "My Father, if it's possible, may this cup be taken from me" (Matthew 26:39).

Jesus knew what was asked of him and what was about to happen if the Father didn't intervene. This wasn't a "cup" he was looking forward to enduring. In fact, we're told his soul was overwhelmed with sorrow to the point of death. Similarities with the scene between Abraham and Isaac are evident. Isaac knew something was up when he asked his father, "The fire and wood are here... but where is the lamb for the burnt offering?" (Genesis 22:7). It's recorded that Abraham responded, "God himself will provide the lamb." Did Abraham further explain, "Isaac, I was told to offer you as a sacrifice, but because of God's promise I have confidence God will resurrect you so you can return with me"? We don't know. Regardless of what was or wasn't said between the two, Isaac would not have looked forward to being bound and sacrificed. The same question Jesus asked of his Father ("Is there any other way?") would have been fitting for Isaac to ask Abraham. Jesus, just as Isaac had done centuries ago, was obedient despite his sorrow and concluded his prayer to the Father, "Yet not as I will, but as you will" (Matthew 26:39).

The answer to Jesus's request comes only moments later. Judas, leading the chief priests and officers of the temple, had just arrived and betrayed Jesus with a kiss. The Father's answer was provided: indeed, it was the only way. It was the way set before the foundation of time and outlined from creation and explained from the time of Moses and through the prophets. It was at this moment that Abraham's words to Isaac, "God himself will provide the lamb," become realized. Yes, it had to be this way.

IT IS FINISHED

It was now the day of Nisan 14. The trials had been completed, and Jesus was sentenced to be crucified. After being mocked, spit upon, beaten, and scourged, the Lamb of God was forced to carry his own cross and was nailed to it. Jesus remained on the cross from about noon to 3 o'clock (Matthew 27:45-46), while, at the same time, the Passover lambs were being sacrificed nearby by the temple officials. It was in that moment:

*... knowing that everything had now been finished, and so that Scripture would be fulfilled, Jesus said, "I am thirsty." A jar of wine vinegar was there, so they soaked a sponge in it, put the sponge on a stalk of the hyssop plant, and lifted it to Jesus' lips. When he had received the drink, Jesus said, "**It is finished**." With that, he bowed his head and gave up his spirit.*

John 19:28-30, emphasis added

At that moment the curtain of the temple was torn in two from top to bottom. The earth shook, the rocks split...

Matthew 27:51

The final barrier that separated man from God was separated in two, just like the Red Sea and the Jordan had been earlier in history. In one remarkable phrase, the Lamb of God declared, *"It is finished."* Then, in conclusion all creation shook.

I am a believer in divine providence. Just as Ruth happened to find herself in Boaz's field, there are many times I just happen to wander into a "field" led by God. One such providential event occurred as I contemplated Jesus's words, *"It is finished,"* and then I came across Scott Hahn's book *The Fourth Cup.*[3] Hahn had been challenged by a pastor to examine the same words, and like I had, he immediately thought the answer was, "It's our redemption that was finished." However, as the pastor noted to Hahn, the work of redemption was not "finished that Friday but at the garden tomb the following Sunday."

So then what was finished?

The clues Hahn explores come from the details of the Last Supper. From our chronology, the Last Supper was before the traditional Passover meal, and was not strictly treated as such. However, as described in the Synoptic Gospels, the meal has many of the same components of a Passover, such as bread and wine.

Many have noted that compared to the four cups of wine at a traditional Passover meal, only three seem to occur at the Last Supper. As Hahn notes[4], the cup Jesus declares "is the blood of the covenant" (Mark 14:24) is likely the third cup, which is known as the cup of redemption.[5]

Rather than finishing the meal with an expected fourth cup of wine, Jesus rather makes an unexpected declaration: "Truly I tell you, I will not drink again from the fruit of the vine until that day when I drink it new in the kingdom of God" (Mark 14:25). He started the meal with many aspects of a Passover as expected by the Disciples, yet he left it unfinished. This variation from the expected is consistent with the events unfolding. Jesus is not overseeing a traditional Passover at all. Rather, he is declaring a new covenant.

Which leads us back to John 19:28. Upon knowing his last breath is coming, Jesus asks for a last drink of wine. Once he has finished that last cup of the Passover, he declares, *"It is finished."* It's the Passover that is finished at that moment and not redemption. The Lamb of God, in this ultimate Passover pointed to from the beginning, finished the Passover once and for all. No longer would the sacrifice need to be repeated endlessly year after year. No longer would blood need to be shed for the covering of sin. The Lamb of God, in one final sacrifice, made a better sacrifice. A sacrifice that was sufficient for all sins.

History also speaks to the completion of Passover. It was only a few years after the crucifixion, when the Jews rebelled against Rome, that the Romans destroyed Jerusalem and the temple in 70 AD. From that point on, for nearly two millennia, there have been no sacrifices of any kind. They were now rendered obsolete.

As we saw from Moses and the law, and then Joshua, and later Ruth, the Passover itself was not the end. It never brought the people into the Promised Land. The Passover was necessary, but it only pointed to the new covenant, to Jesus, who would complete redemption by providing rest. The culmination of those Passover events, and the completion of redemption were to still to come. Early the next Sunday morning, we're told:

He is not here; he has risen!   Luke 24:6

Final redemption and rest were completed through the resurrection, not the death. It's through the resurrection that the final layers of redemption from Exodus 6:2-8, our being *carried* and *received* into fellowship with God, were completed.

ONE COMPLETE STORY FROM THE BEGINNING

We started this journey with a desire to explore the coherency of God's plan of redemption through the Passover up to Easter. When I look at the Passover, its entire plan, from creation to the resurrection, I see the most remarkable and coherent plan imaginable.

There are times, such as the season of Lent, when it's appropriate to go back in detail through all the stories, shadows, and imagery and to walk the entire story again. Or, as I described in the opening chapters, to meet Jesus again for the first time.

There are also times when the details don't need to be explored exhaustively, but the journey only needs to be relived as in a picture album. I find myself in the latter case whenever I partake of communion as a remembrance of the Last Supper, when I hear of redemption, and, of course, during Easter. Looking at the entire story from the beginning at a high level is quite remarkable. Summarizing the journey takes us down the following path:

From "the beginning was the Word, and the Word was with God, and the Word was God" (John 1:1) …

to the creation of the moon to mark *this* day …

to the first blood sacrifice to "cover" sin in the garden …

to Isaac, Abraham's only son whom he loved, carrying the wood himself with obedience to death …

to the first Passover with the blood of a lamb …

to Joshua and the arrival in the Promised Land …

to Ruth and the promise of rest and redemption …

to Jesus approaching Jerusalem with the Passover lambs just hours before the tenth day of Nisan as people were yelling "Hosanna," or "Save us," as the Lamb of God called "Yahweh is Salvation," rides toward his destiny…

to four days of inspection resulting in the declaration of the Lamb of God being without defect…

to being crucified at the same time as the Passover lambs…

to the figurative and literal curtain in the temple being torn from above as the promise was completed…

to the declaration that He has risen!

That is the Passover—the story of Easter from the beginning!

To me, that journey indeed answers the call to, "Restore to me the joy of your salvation and grant me a willing spirit, to sustain me" (Psalm 51:12).

A fitting conclusion to this journey comes from Melito of Sardis. He writes:

> *"So come all families of people,*
> *adulterated with sin.*
> *For I am your freedom.*
> *I am the Passover Salvation,*
> *I am the lamb slaughtered for you,*
> *I am your ransom,*
> *I am your life,*
> *I am your light,*
> *I am your salvation,*
> *I am your resurrection,*
> *I am your King.*
> *I shall raise you up by my hand,*
> *I will lead you to the heights of heaven,*
> *there shall I show you the everlasting father."*

Melito of Sardis[6]

Grace and peace to you. He is risen!

-NOTES-

Chapter 1: Puzzle Pieces

[1] The word "departure" is Strong's G1841, *exodos*, which means "an exit." It occurs three times in the New Testament. First, here in Luke 9:31. But also in Hebrews 11:22, where it is translated as "exodus "and finally in 2 Peter 1:15.

[2] N.E.Thing Enterprises, *Magic Eye: A New Way of Looking at the World*, Andrews and McMeel Publishing; 1st edition, 1993.

[3] Jayson Georges, *The 3D Gospel: Ministry in Guilt, Shame, and Fear Cultures*, Time Press, 2017.

[4] Eugene Nida, *Customs and Cultures*, Harper, 1954. This division of culture was initiated by Nida, then expanded and popularized by Roland Muller in *Honor and Shame: Unlocking the Door*, Xlibris, 2001.

Chapter 2: What's in a Name?

[1] German uses *Ostern* to refer to Easter. Along with English, it derives Easter from the name of the pagan goddess, Eostre. Most other languages don't. Some translate our Easter as "resurrection" such as Japanese—*Fukkatsu-sai* (literally "resurrection festival") and Serbian—*Vaskrs* or *Uskrs* (literally "resurrection"). A few others use "grand day" or "night," such as Slovak—Velka Noc (literally "grand night").

[2] Bob Seidensticker, "10 Reasons the Crucifixion Story Makes No Sense," http://www.patheos.com/blogs/crossexamined/2012/04/10-reasons-the-crucifixion-story-makes-no-sense/, Published: April 8, 2012.

3 Daniel Peterson, "Defending the Faith: Are there any good reasons to believe?", https://www.deseretnews.com/article/900009262/are-there-any-good-reasons-to-believe.html, Published: February 2, 2018.

4 The name "Kenan" is Strong's H7018 and is often interpreted as "possession," derived from its similarity with "Canaan." However, there is some uncertainty in its meaning. It is also derived from the Hebrew קֵינָן which can also mean "sorrow" or "dirge."

5 Genesis 1:26, 27; Genesis 2:5, 7, 8, 15, 16, 18, 19.

6 This list was adapted from: Dr. Chuck Missler, *Cosmic Codes: Hidden Messages From the Edge of Eternity*, Koinonia House, 1999, pp. 72-75

Chapter 3: The First Passover

1 *Hayah* is Strong's H1961, which means: to be, become, come to pass, exist, happen, fall out.

2 Kenneth E. Bailey, *Jesus Through Middle Eastern Eyes*, IVP Academic, 2008, pp. 13-18.

3 Some examples include Psalm 23 and Isaiah 28:8-14.

4 The term "giving" appears twice. First, in reference to the covenant, and before the patriarchs are named. Second, after the patriarchs are named, and, to reinforce that the land was given as a gift.

5 Baruch Bokser, *Origins of the Seder*, Univ. of California Press, 1984.

6 There are many other less common attempts to explain why four cups are used. Some include their corresponding to the four times that the Torah refers to the cup of Pharaoh (Genesis 40). One tradition links each cup with one of the four matriarchs—Sarah, Rebekah, Rachel and Leah—who gave birth to the Jewish people.

7 Eliyaho Kitov, *The Book of Our Heritage*, 3 volumes (Feldheim, 1988), 2.269

8 Or a goat. The word can mean both. This idea is further emphasized by verse 5.

9 The Hebrew word *aviv* (Heb. אביב) actually translates as the season of "spring." We find mention of the "month of Aviv" several times in the biblical writings. An example is in Exodus

13:4, which reads, "Today you are going out, in the month of Aviv." The use of "spring" emphasizes that the Passover will always coincide with the right season, during the aviv, spring. After the Babylonian exile there were two calendars: the civil calendar as the official calendar of kings, and the religious one used to calculate the dates of the feasts and festivals. As a result, the first month is referred to as "Aviv" in the civil calendar and alternatively as "Nisan" in the religious calendar. Aviv and Nisan are often used interchangeably when talking about the Passover.

[10] Humphreys goes into great deal about the lunar calendar, its history, and how it was practically implemented in a book by Colin Humphreys, *The Mystery of the Last Supper: Reconstructing the Final Days of Jesus*, Cambridge University Press, 2011.

[11] *Moed* is Strong's H4150 and is, properly, an appointed sign or time, i.e., a fixed time or season; specifically, a festival and, by implication, an assembly (as convened for a definite purpose). Other examples occur in Genesis. 17:21 and Genesis 18:14.

Chapter 4: Genesis — From the Beginning

[1] Some examples include: when Pharaoh pursued the Israelites just hours after leaving (Exodus 14:11-12); complaining about the bitter water (Exodus 15:22); and complaining about being hungry and God providing them Manna (Exodus 16:1-4).

[2] Also in Hebrews 8:7-10 (quoting Jeremiah 31:32-34).

[3] *Kaphar* is Strong's H3722, which means "to cover," "purge," "make an atonement," "make reconciliation," and "cover over with pitch." It is translated as "atonement" 71 times.

[4] The next time is in Genesis 27:16, when Rebekah covers Jacob's hand with goatskins. The second mention of *owr* with regard to animal hides is in Exodus 25:5, when Moses is told to collect ram skins for the tabernacle.

[5] The word used here for love is *ahab* and is its first appearance. The word "love" appears in our translations earlier such as "make love" (Genesis 4:1,17,25) but it's a different Hebrew word, *yada*, meaning "relations" or "be familiar with." "Love" also appears in Genesis 20:13, but it too is a different Hebrew word, *hesed* or *checed*, which means faithfulness.

⁶ The Greek word in the New Testament is derived from *agapaō* which means "to love," as in a person or thing. In Hebrew, *ahab*, is also used in the context of human love. Though they are different languages, they both refer to the same love.

⁷ According to Jewish tradition Sarah died after hearing about what had happened. Since she dies at 127 and Isaac was born when she was 90, he would have been 36 or 37 years old. However, in the writings of Josephus, the age of Isaac at the time, is said to be twenty-five years old. (Antiquities of the Jews: English (1.13.2)). The word used for boy in Genesis 22:5 in speaking of Isaac is very flexible and is also used for Ishmael in Genesis 21:18, when he was about 18 years old.

⁸ Beersheba is approximately 65 miles southwest of Mount Moriah and is the likely start since they return there at the end of Genesis 22.

⁹ *Eliezer* is from Strong's H410 ("God of help"), and H5828 ("helper"), used of Eve in Genesis 2:18.

Chapter 5: Joshua and the Passover

¹ *Yĕshuwah* is Strong's H3444 ("Something saved, i.e. (abstractly) deliverance; hence, aid, victory, prosperity: — deliverance").

² Exodus 12:48.

³ In Numbers 20:8, when the Israelites complained about having no water, the Lord told Moses to speak to the rock and it would pour out its water. In Numbers 20:10-11, Moses struck the rock twice with his staff rather than speaking to it as the Lord had commanded. In response the Lord said, "Because you did not trust in me enough to honor me as holy in the sight of the Israelites, you will not bring this community into the land I give them" (Numbers 20:12). Such a public example of direct disobedience could not go unpunished. It also seems that God had intended to present a type of Christ in this circumstance. The water-giving rock is used as a symbol of Christ in 1 Corinthians 10:4. The rock was struck once in Exodus 17:6, just like Christ was crucified once (Hebrews 7:27). Moses's speaking to the rock in Numbers 20 was to be a picture of prayer.

4 Gilgal is a word play that takes advantage of the root *gll* for "to roll," which sounds like the name Gilgal.

5 *Cherpah* is Strong's H2778: "disgrace, rebuke, reproach(-fully)." It also occurs in Genesis 30:23 and 1 Samuel 17:26 and is used in a similar manner.

6 In Numbers 15:38, Moses was told to "Speak to the Israelites and say to them: 'Throughout the generations to come you are to make tassels on the corners of your garments, with a blue cord on each tassel.' " The reason was so, "you will remember all the commands of the LORD." The special blue color was called *tekhelet*. In ancient times, blue was one of the most expensive colors to produce, which made these blue threads very valuable and important. They represented royalty as well as the heavens and divinity.

7 Joshua 1:6, 8, 9.

Chapter 6: Redemption, Rest, and Ruth

1 The first fruits, a sheaf of barley, which is offered in connection with the Feast of Unleavened Bread (Leviticus 23:9-14), directly following the Passover, and the first fruits of the second harvest, the loaves of bread, which are offered at Pentecost, were both wave offerings. The sheaf of barley to be reaped was marked out by delegates from the Sanhedrim, who tied them together in bundles before the Passover. Later, after the Passover, in a ceremony, the delegates first asked the bystanders three times each of these questions: "Has the sun gone down?"; "With this sickle?"; "Into this basket?"; "On this Sabbath?"; and, lastly, "Shall I reap?" After the questions were answered by the bystanders, they cut down barley to the amount of one ephah or about three pints, and brought it into the temple. *The Jewish Encyclopedia: A Descriptive Record of the History, Religion, Literature, and Customs of the Jewish People from the Earliest Times to the Present Day*, Volume 5, p. 396.

2 Though some form of a written Pentateuch is quite old, it would only have been available to priests. Even much later, at the time of Ezra the Scribe (c. 537 BCE), when public reading of the Torah was introduced, the Torah scrolls were not available to common people. Naomi's account of her heritage would have been passed down based on oral tradition.

3 In Ruth 1:20, Naomi contrasts the meaning of her name, which means "pleasant," with the word *mara* meaning "bitter." Arthur Cundall, *Judges and Ruth: An Introduction and Commentary*, Intervarsity Press, 2008.

4 Also Ruth 2:20 (third occurrence of *hesed* in Ruth)

5 *Hesed* is Strong's H2617: "kindness; by implication (towards God, good, loving-kindness, mercy." The most common translations are: mercy (149x), kindness (40x), lovingkindness (30x), and goodness (12x). A good discussion of *hesed* and Ruth is provided by Carolyn Custis James in a chapter she calls "The Power of Hesed" in *The Gospel of Ruth*, Zondervan, 2008, pp 109-123.

6 Deuteronomy 5:10, 7:9, 7:12.

7 Carolyn Custis James, The Gospel of Ruth, Zondervan, 2008, p 115.

8 Jude has "mercy and peace." Hebrews, James and 1 John don't open with "grace and peace."

9 Carolyn Custis James, op. cit., p. 112.

10 In Matthew 1:5 it's recorded that Rahab was Boaz's mother, with the implication that she was married to Salmon. The genealogy in the last chapter of Ruth spans from Perez (the son of Judah, who was a brother of Joseph) to David which covers approximately 650 years. However, only ten names are listed. It's likely this genealogy is only a summary and somewhat compressed. In such a case, Rahab was likely a great-grandmother or great-great-grandmother of Boaz. This is similar to when Jacob calls Abraham his father in Genesis 32:9, although he is his grandfather. A discussion of the genealogy is provided in Arthur Cundall, *Judges and Ruth: An Introduction and Commentary*, Intervarsity Press, 2008.

11 *Shachath* is Strong's H7843 and is translated in the following manner: destroy (96x), corrupt (22x), mar (7x), destroyer (3x), corrupters (2x).

12 Arthur Cundall, op. cit., p 297.

Chapter 7: Timing of the Last Supper

1 Also included within Passion Week are Holy Monday, Holy Tuesday, Spy Wednesday, Maundy Thursday, Good Friday, and Holy Saturday.

2 Tacitus Annals, XV, 44.

3 This is explained in many ways, one of which is the adherence to the Johannine interpretation of events where the meal was held before the Passover.

4 Joachim Jeremias, *The Eucharist Words of Jesus*, Trinity Press International, 1966, Eighth impression, 1990.

5 The fourteen points that Jeremias provide supporting the Last Supper as a Passover meal are: 1. The Last Supper took place in Jerusalem; 2. The upper room was made freely available to the Disciples; 3. It took place at night; 4. Jesus celebrated the Last Supper with only the twelve Disciples; 5. They reclined at the table; 6. The meal was eaten in a state of Levitical purity; 7. Jesus broke bread during the course of the meal; 8. Jesus and the Disciples drank wine at the Last Supper; 9. The wine was red; 10. The Disciples assumed that Judas left to make last-minute purchases for the festival; 11. They assumed that Judas had been commissioned to give something to the poor; 12. The Last Supper ended with the singing of hymns; 13. After the meal Jesus did not return to Bethany; 14. Jesus spoke words of interpretation over the bread and wine. In the eighth impression from 1990, these are on pages 42-56.

6 The ten points of objection that Jeremias provide to the Last Supper being a Passover meal, and then refutes, are: 1. Mark 14:22 speaks of "bread," whereas only "unleavened bread" would be used for a Passover; 2. The early Church repeated the Last Supper daily; 3. No reference is made to the Passover ritual such as bitter herbs and a lamb; 4. The description of the Last Supper is inconsistent with the Passover ritual; 5. The Sanhedrin did not want to arrest Jesus during the feast (Mark 14:2); 6. Mark 15:6 mentions the Passover amnesty where a prisoner would be released before the Passover; 7. Paul, in 1 Corinthians 5:7b, refers to Christ as the Passover Lamb; 8. In 1 Corinthians 15:20, Christ is referred to as the "first fruits," which supports the crucifixion on Nisan 14 and the resurrection on Nisan 16; 9. Many of the incidents reported could not have taken place on Nisan 15; 10. The chief objection is the Johannine account. In the eighth impression from 1990, these are on pages 62-84.

7 Josephus in *The Jewish War 6.9.3* claims 2,700,000 people were in Jerusalem for the Passover, which required 256,500 lambs to be slaughtered. However, most scholars view this number as highly

exaggerated. Sanders in *Judaism: Practice and Belief 63 BCE-66 CE* estimates that there were only 300,000 to 500,000 people. Jeremias in *The Eucharist Words of Jesus* (p. 42), estimates just over 100,000 people were in Jerusalem for the Passover at the time, requiring no more than 15,000 lambs.

8 Annie Jaubert, *The date of the Last Supper,* Staten Island, NY, Alba House, 1965.

9 The Book of Jubilees and the Didascalia Apostolorum.

10 Pope Benedict XVI, *Jesus of Nazareth: Holy Week: From the Entrance Into Jerusalem To The Resurrection*, Ignatius Press, 2001, pp 106-114.

11 Jonathan Klawans, *Was Jesus' Last Supper a Seder?*, Bible Review, October 2001.

12 C. Humphreys, *The Mystery of the Last Supper: Reconstructing the Final Days of Jesus*, Cambridge University Press, 2011.

13 J Meier, *A Marginal Jew: Rethinking the Historical Jesus*, Doubleday, 1991.

14 Scott Hahn, *The Fourth Cup: Unveiling the Mystery of the Last Supper and the Cross*, Image, 2018.

15 Formally the Passover had to occur after the Vernal Equinox which sets some of the official details of the lunar calendar and intercalation.

16 Joachim Jeremias, op. cit., pp 36-41.

17 J.K. Fotheringham, *The Evidence of Astronomy and Technical Chronology for the Date of the Crucifixion*, The Journal of Theological Studies, vol. 35, 1934.

18 Joachim Jeremias, op. cit., pp 36-37.

19 C. Humphreys, op. cit., pp 39-60.

20 It occurred on either Nisan 14 or 15 in both AD 27 and AD 34. However, AD 27 is excluded because it required a delay of a day due to poor visibility and is regarded as too early by many due to Luke's account of John the Baptist's ministry (Luke 3:1-2). Additionally, AD 34 is excluded because it is considered too late based on the date of Paul's conversion.

21 Joachim Jeremias, op. cit., p 41.

22 Humphreys and Waddington, *Dating the Crucifixion*, Nature, vol. 306, 1983.

23 Pope Benedict XVI, op. cit.

Chapter 8: Face to Face with the Lamb of God

[1] Jeremias in *The Eucharist Words of Jesus* (p. 42), estimates between 110,000 and 155,000 people were in Jerusalem for Passover at the time. Assuming ten people per household would require between 11,000 and 15,500 lambs.

[2] "This Is the Day," Lead Me, Guide Me (2nd ed.), #305

[3] Scott Hahn, *The Fourth Cup: Unveiling the Mystery of the Last Supper and the Cross*, Image, 2018.

[4] Scott Hahn, op. cit., p. 109.

[5] It must be noted that many scholars doubt that the traditions of the current Seder we know, such as the four cups, can be proven to exist at the time of Jesus. The first records of Seders only occur at the end of the first century. In spite of this uncertainty, it's probable that many of the traditions were in place in some sense. In Baruck Bokser's book *The Origins of the Seder*, he demonstrates that most rabbinic traditions can be traced back to just after the destruction of the temple in AD 70.

[6] Melito, *On Pascha: With the Fragments of Melito and Other Material Related to the Quartodecimans*, St Vladimirs Seminary Pr, 2001, p. 66.

38031715R00086

Made in the USA
Middletown, DE
04 March 2019